Contents

Acknowledgment

The designs in this book were originally featured in *Woman's Weekly* magazine and my sincere thanks are due to the editor and all home department staff for their kind co-operation during the preparation of the book.

I also wish to thank Pauline Stride of Batsford for her constant helpfulness and efficiency.

SMALL CUDDLY TOYS

SMALL CUDDLY TOYS

Jean Greenhowe

 Sterling Publishing Co., Inc.   New York

Library of Congress Cataloging in Publication Data

Greenhowe, Jean.
  Small cuddly toys.

  1. Toy making. 2. Soft toy making. I. Title.
TT174G717 1874   745.592′4   84-23994
ISBN 0-8069-5710-7
ISBN 0-8069-7988-7 (pbk.)

Introduction

In this book there are patterns and full instructions for making over fifty items, including soft toys, animals, dolls, mascot toys and puppets as well as a feature on modelling miniatures from bread dough. The toys range from those which are quick to make, like the pencil toppers, to more elaborate designs such as the baby doll in a fabric-lined basket with a complete layette of clothes.

Several of the dolls and animals are constructed from circles of fabric gathered into rosettes and threaded onto lengths of elastic. I myself find these rosette toys extremely enjoyable to make since the circles can be cut out and gathered at any odd moment, almost like doing patchwork. Hansel, Gretel and the witch and Santa and Mrs Claus are made in this way as well as a whole set of miniature jungle animals.

All the toys are economical of materials, requiring only remnants of fabrics and trimmings plus household odds and ends.

General instructions

Materials

Most of the materials used for the toys in this book can be found in the rag bag or around the house. Rag bag remnants and dressmaking cuttings are particularly useful for making the rosette toys since the fabric circles can be cut from a variety of different fabrics if desired.

Fawn fleecy fabric is required for making many of the soft toys and animals. This man-made fibre fabric is knitted and is therefore slightly stretchy, with a soft brushed surface. It is extremely suitable for making very small animals since the furry pile does not obscure the detail, as would be the case if normal fur fabric were used. Fleecy fabric is sold for making things like dressing gowns and toys, and most good fabric shops stock a variety of colours besides fawn or beige.

For stuffing the soft toys, kapok, washable man-made fibre stuffing or even cotton wool (cotton ball) can be used.

Round elastic is required for making the rosette toys. This type of elastic, sometimes known as hat elastic, is obtainable in different thicknesses. Elastic of about 2 mm ($\frac{1}{16}$in.) in diameter is about the right thickness.

Gluing

The adhesive used should be an all-purpose quick drying type such as UHU or Elmer's Glue. Apply very small amounts of adhesive with the point of a pin or needle. When sticking (i.e. gluing) an item together, unwanted smears of this adhesive can be removed by dabbing carefully with a cloth dipped in acetone. Take care when using acetone as it is highly inflammable.

When cutting out tiny pieces of felt, the cut edges tend to be fluffy and indistinct. To counteract this, spread the back of the felt with adhesive, smooth it into the felt with the fingertips, then leave to dry. When cut out, the shapes will have well-defined edges.

Tools

A ruler and pair of compasses are required for drawing out rectangular and circular patterns as quoted in the instructions. When cutting out tiny felt shapes use small sharp needlework scissors.

Although not essential, a leather punch if available is ideal for punching out perfect felt circles for doll and animal eyes. The felt should first be treated with adhesive as already mentioned.

Patterns, sewing and cutting out

The patterns are all printed full size on the pages except for one or two shapes which are too large to fit on the page. These are given as simple diagrams with measurements. Patterns can be traced off the pages onto thin writing paper, then the details should be marked onto each pattern piece.

All fabric pieces should be seamed with the right sides of the fabric together unless otherwise stated. Seam allowances are given in the instructions for each toy.

After sewing seams in fur fabric or fleece, pick out the pile trapped in the seams on the right side of the fabric with the point of a pin.

When embroidering facial features on a toy, start and finish the sewing threads at a place which will be hidden on the finished toy. For example under the position of a felt eye or nose, or at the back of a doll's head.

Before cutting out pieces of stockinette or cotton knit, test the fabric by pulling, to find the direction in which the fabric stretches the most. Cut out the pieces placing the 'most stretch' in the direction indicated on the pattern or in the instructions.

Safety in toys

When making toys for children it is just as important to consider the safety factor as it is when buying toys. Very young children in particular should not be given toys containing wire, buttons, beads or any other items which could be dangerous, or detached and swallowed.

Measurements

All the sizes in this book have been worked out separately in both centimetres and inches, so that in many instances the measurements given do not accurately convert from one to the other. This has been done in order to avoid having awkward sizes when in fact a little extra either way makes no difference to the finished toy. The toymaker can use either metric or imperial, following one or the other throughout on each toy.

How to make
the stitch-around toys

Many of the toys in this book are made by a simple stitch-around method as shown in the diagram here. The paper pattern is traced off the page and cut out, then it is pinned onto two layers of fabric. The toy is then stitched all round through both layers of fabric close to the edges of the paper pattern, leaving a gap in the seam for turning. After removing the pattern, the toy is cut out close to the stitching line then turned right side out. This method makes the accurate seaming together of very small pattern pieces an easy matter.

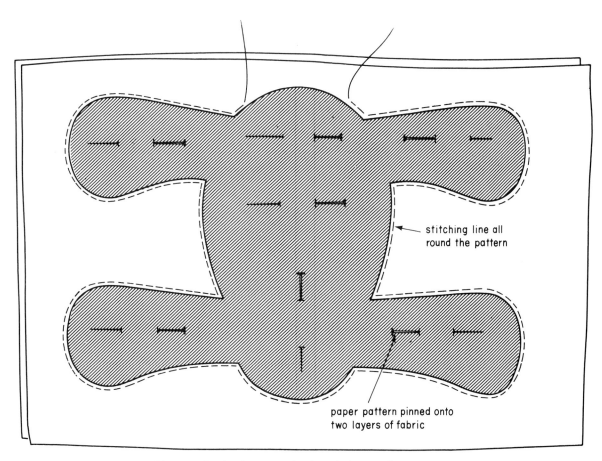

stitching line all round the pattern

paper pattern pinned onto two layers of fabric

Diagram showing how to make the stitch-around toys

How to make the rosette toys

Thin card, cut from cereal or washing powder boxes etc, is required for making the circle templates. Draw out the circles with compasses to the sizes given in the instructions for each rosette toy. Cut out the card circles then mark the size of the diameter on each one. All the card circles should be stored away after completing a particular toy because some of the same size circles can probably be used for another toy.

Now draw round one of the card circles onto a piece of fabric, then cut out the fabric circle. If a number of circles of the same size are required,

several can be cut at the same time as follows. Pin the cut out fabric circle close to the edges all round onto three or four layers of fabric. Cut out all the circles even with the edge of the first circle.

Fold each circle into quarters and snip off the corner at the centre to make a tiny hole as shown in the diagram. Run a gathering thread all round the edge of the circle then pull up the gathers until the raw edges meet and fasten off. Flatten the gathered circle into a rosette having the gathers lying on top of the centre hole.

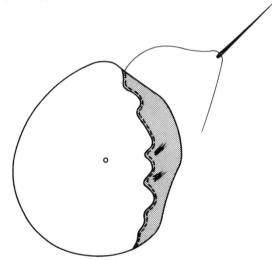

snip off this corner

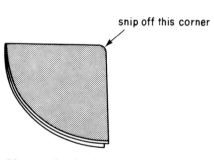

Diagram showing the fabric circle folded into quarters

Diagram showing the fabric circle being gathered

Diagram showing a finished rosette

12

Two little dolls, sleeping baby and Victorian miss

The baby and Victorian miss are about 30 cm (12 in.) in length. They are easy to make using a baby sock for the head and hands with gathered rosettes of fabric for the bodice and sleeves. No legs are required beneath their long skirts and each can be used as a simple hand puppet by slipping the skirt over the hand and grasping the button at the waist. One type of fabric only has been used for each doll illustrated but remnants of various fabrics can be used if desired.

Seams and turnings of 1 cm (⅜ in.) are allowed unless otherwise stated. Make the fabric rosettes as given at the beginning of the book.

Materials required for each doll
One pink or white smallest size baby sock with plain-knit foot (note that white can be tinted pink if desired)
Thin round elastic, 50 cm (20 in.) in length

(Left) Victorian miss, (right) sleeping baby

Scraps of knitting wool, black felt, black and pink thread and red pencil

White fabric, 50 cm (20 in.) long and 91 cm (36 in.) wide, for the baby; printed fabric, 60 cm (24 in.) long and 91 cm (36 in.) wide for Victorian miss; or remnants of fabric as mentioned previously.

Narrow lace edging for baby, or narrow ribbon for Victorian miss, 1.1 m (1¼ yd) in length

Short length of narrow ribbon and lace edging

Stuffing

One button about 2 cm (¾ in.) in diameter with two or four holes through the centre

To make the baby doll

For the head, stuff the toe end of the sock firmly to make a ball-shape, measuring about 16 cm (6¼ in.) in circumference. Run a gathering thread round the sock just below the stuffing, then cut across the sock 5 mm (¼ in.) below the gathering thread. Lay aside the cut off piece of sock to use later on for making the hands. Turn in the 5 mm (¼ in.) and pull up the gathers slightly.

Cut a 30 cm (12 in.) length of elastic, then fold it in half and knot the folded end. Push the knot inside the head and pull up the gathering thread tightly. Fasten off the thread, oversewing through the elastic to hold it securely in place. Work two shallow U-shapes for the eyes in black stitches about half way down the face and 1 cm (⅜ in.) apart. Work black stitches for the eyelashes and use pink thread to work tiny stitches for the mouth and nose as shown in the illustration. Colour the cheeks by rubbing with the moistened tip of the red pencil. For the hair sew a few short lengths of teased out wool to the forehead.

For the bonnet cut an 11 cm (4¼ in.) diameter circle of fabric, turn in the raw edges 5 mm (¼ in.) and tack. Sew lace edging round the edge of the bonnet with small running stitches. Pull up the thread until the bonnet fits on the baby's head as shown, then fasten off the thread. Sew the bonnet to the baby's head all round through the gathers.

For the baby gown cut and gather twenty-six 7 cm (2¾ in.) diameter circles of fabric and one 12 cm (4¾ in.) diameter circle.

For one hand cut a 4 cm (1½ in.) square off the remaining piece of sock. Fold it in half and join the raw edges, tacking a tiny seam, leaving one 4 cm (1½ in.) edge open and rounding off the remaining corners. Trim off the corners, turn the hand right side out and stuff. Run a gathering thread round the hand 5 mm (¼ in.) from the raw edge. Turn in the raw edge and pull up the gathers tightly enclosing the knotted end of a 20 cm (8 in.) length of elastic for

the arms. Oversew through the elastic to hold it in place. Cut a 15 cm (6 in.) length of narrow lace edging, join the ends, then gather it up for a wrist frill, and thread it onto the arm elastic. Now thread ten small gathered circles onto the arm elastic, thus forming one sleeve.

Thread three small gathered circles onto the head elastics, then pass the arm elastic between the two head elastics. Thread three more small circles onto the head elastics. Complete the other sleeve by threading the remaining ten circles onto the arm elastic. Make the wrist frill and the hand, and sew the hand in place as for the other hand, shortening the elastic as necessary.

For the underskirt cut a 24 cm by 45 cm (9½ in. by 18 in.) strip of fabric. Join the short edges, then hem one remaining raw edge. Turn in the other raw edge 5 mm (¼ in.), run round a gathering thread, pull up tightly then fasten off the thread.

For the overskirt cut a 25 cm by 45 cm (10 in. by 18 in.) strip of fabric. Make it as for the underskirt, trimming the hem edge with lace edging.

Pass the head elastics through the gathered end of the skirt, through the gathered end of the underskirt, then through the 12 cm (4¾ in.) diameter gathered circle. Finally pass each elastic through a separate hole in the button, then knot the ends together securely and trim off any excess elastic.

Make a ribbon bow and sew it to the fabric circle below the chin as illustrated.

To make the Victorian miss

Make as for the baby with the following exceptions. For the hair, sew the centres of a few 20 cm (8 in.) long strands of wool to the forehead. Take the strands down the sides of the head and sew them there, then take them to the back of the head and sew the ends in place. Sew a few loops of wool to the forehead for a fringe.

Cut tiny circles of black felt for the eyes and sew them in place with a single stitch taken through the centre of each eye to the back of the head, pulling the thread tightly each time. For the hat use a 13 cm (5 in.) diameter circle of fabric. Make as for the baby's bonnet, trimming the edge with ribbon, then put a little stuffing in the hat to shape it before sewing it to the head. Sew a ribbon bow to the front of the hat.

Cut thirty-six circles for the bodice and sleeves and use eight for the bodice and fourteen for each sleeve. Use ribbon for the wrist frills and for trimming the hem edge of the skirt. Add a little frill of lace edging round the neck.

The three little kittens

Here is a group of toys representing the nursery rhyme 'Three little kittens lost their mittens'. Mother cat is 15 cm (6 in.) high and each kitten measures 11 cm (4¼ in.). The kittens wear little felt mittens which are colour-matched to their dresses. All the clothes are sewn in place except for the mittens.

Mother and kittens are all made from the same basic patterns using the stitch-around method. Seams and turnings of 3 mm (⅛ in.) are allowed on all other pieces unless otherwise stated.

Materials required
Pink fleecy fabric, 20 cm (8 in.) long and 122 cm (48 in.) wide
Small amount of stuffing

Broderie Anglaise (or eyelet) edging, 1.8 m (2 yd) long and 4 cm (1½ in.) wide

Scraps of fabrics, lace edging, guipure (lace) flower trimming, felt and card (thin cardboard)

For the facial features, scraps of black and pink felt, black thread and red pencil

For the pie, brown felt, stuffing, brown pencil and a small metal lid off a coffee or cocoa tin

For the table, a small cardboard box, white fabric and lace edging

Adhesive

To make a kitten

Trace the body, base and arm patterns off the page onto thin paper. Cut out the patterns then trim the body and arm patterns along the dotted lines indicated on these patterns. Pin the body pattern onto two layers of fleecy fabric having the right sides of the fabric together. Cut the fabric even with the pattern at the lower edges. Now machine stitch all round close to the edge of the paper pattern leaving the lower edges open. Remove the pattern and cut out the kitten close to the stitching line. Turn right side out. Work a running stitch through both thicknesses of fabric at the base of each ear as shown on the pattern.

Cut the base from card then stick it to the wrong side of a piece of fleecy fabric. Cut out the fabric 5 mm (¼ in.) larger all round than the card. Turn and

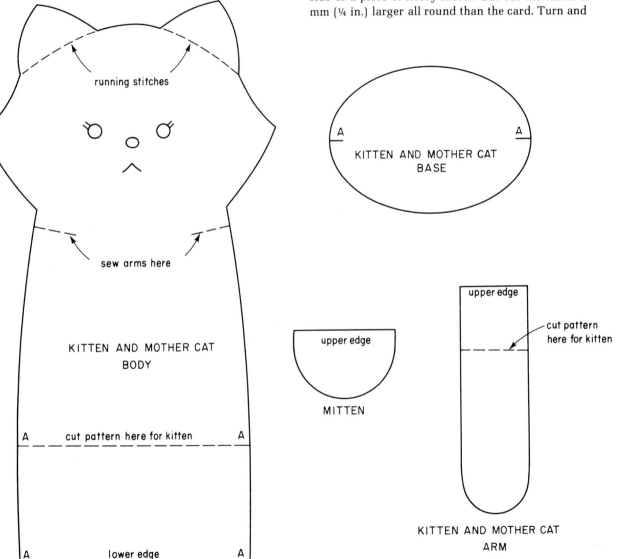

running stitches

sew arms here

KITTEN AND MOTHER CAT
BODY

A   cut pattern here for kitten   A

A   lower edge   A

KITTEN AND MOTHER CAT
BASE

A   A

upper edge

MITTEN

upper edge

cut pattern here for kitten

KITTEN AND MOTHER CAT
ARM

glue this extra fabric to the other side of the card. Stuff the kitten then place the base against the lower raw edges of the kitten matching points A. Oversew the lower raw edge to the edge of the base all round adding more stuffing if necessary before completing the sewing. Now tie a double strand of sewing thread as tightly as possible round the kitten's neck then sew the ends of the thread into the neck.

Cut the eyes from black felt and the nose from pink felt as shown on the pattern then glue them in place. Work small stitches for the eyelashes and mouth using black thread. Colour the cheeks by rubbing with the moistened tip of a red pencil. Sew a ribbon bow to the top of the head as illustrated.

Pin the arm pattern onto two layers of fleecy fabric having the right sides of the fabric together. Trim the fabric even with the upper edge of the pattern. Stitch, cut out and turn in the same way as for the body leaving the upper edges open. Stuff the lower part of the arms only, then oversew the upper edges together. Do not sew the arms to the body at this stage.

For the kitten's dress cut a 7.5 cm by 20 cm (3 in. by 8 in.) strip of fabric. Turn in and glue one long edge to neaten, then join the short edges. Turn the dress right side out, then turn in the remaining raw edge and run a gathering thread round it. Put the dress on the kitten having the seam at the centre back. Pull up the gathers round the neck and fasten off. Now oversew the tops of the arms to the kitten at each side at the positions shown on the pattern, taking the stitches through the dress and into the fleecy fabric.

For the apron cut 30 cm (12 in.) of Broderie Anglaise (eyelet) edging. Join the short edges, then turn in the raw edge and run round a gathering thread. Put the apron on the kitten under the arms having the seam at the centre back. Pull up the thread having the gathered edge about 2 cm (¾ in.) down from the neck edge of the dress. Finish off the thread then sew the gathered edge of the apron to the dress all round.

For the apron shoulder frill, cut a 30 cm (12 in.) strip of edging, then join the short edges. Turn in the raw edge 1 cm (⅜ in.) and run round a gathering

'Lost your mittens. you naughty kitten!'

thread. Put the frill round the kitten's neck having the seam at the centre back. Pull up the gathers so that the frill touches the neck at the back and dips down at the centre front as shown in the illustration. Finish off the thread and sew the gathered edge of the frill in place. Catch the frill to the apron at the back. Sew a tiny ribbon bow to the frill at the front.

To make a mitten, cut two mitten pieces from felt to match the kitten's dress. Oversew the curved edges of the mitten together leaving the upper edges open. Turn the mitten right side out and stretch it slightly over a fingertip or the blunt end of a pencil so that it will fit easily over the kitten's hand. Glue on a small guipure (lace) flower, then make the other mitten in the same way.

To make mother cat

Trace the full size body and arm patterns off the page, then make them in the same way as for the kitten. Make the eyes, nose and mouth as for the kitten, but place the eyes a little higher up the face and closer together.

For the dress cut a 10.5 cm by 22 cm (4⅛ in. by 8¾ in.) strip of fabric. Make it and sew it in place as for the kitten's dress. For one dress sleeve cut a 5 cm by 9 cm (2 in. by 3½ in.) strip of fabric. Join the short edges then turn in the remaining raw edges and run a gathering thread round one of them. Put the sleeves on the arm and pull up the gathered edge at the top of the arm, the finish off, oversewing the sleeve to the top of the arm. Sew lace edging round the remaining edge of the sleeve using small running stitches. Pull up the stitches to fit the arm then finish off. Make the other sleeve in the same way, then sew the arms in place as for the kitten. Gather a small frill of lace edging round the neck to match the sleeves. Tie a length of ribbon round the dress for a sash as illustrated, fastening it in a bow at the back.

For the hat cut a 12 cm (4¾ in.) diameter circle of fabric. Turn in the raw edge and sew on lace edging with small running stitches. Pull up the stitches to make the hat fit on the head as illustrated, then fasten off the thread. Stuff the hat, then sew it in place on the head, taking the stitches through the gathers all round. Sew a ribbon bow to the front of the hat.

To make the table

Cut a piece of fabric to fit over the cardboard box covering it completely as illustrated. Glue lace edging round the edge of the fabric then glue the tablecloth to the box.

To make the pie

For the pie crust cut a circle of light brown felt a little larger all round than the metal lid. Stretch the centre of the felt circle a little, then fold the circle in half and make three small snips at the centre in the same way as for a real pie crust. Glue a small piece of brown fabric or felt underneath the snips. Put a little stuffing in the centre of the metal lid and spread adhesive all round the rim. Place the pie crust on top of the lid pressing the edge in place all round. Trim the felt even with the edge of the lid if necessary. Colour the crust here and there by rubbing with moistened brown pencil for a well-baked effect.

To make the crimped effect round the edge of the pie, use the edge of a hot iron close to the point of the iron, pressing it into the felt at regular intervals all round. Gently iron the pie crust all over to smooth the felt.

Humpty Dumpty game

The aim of this game is to knock the three Humpty Dumptys off the wall by throwing three small balls of wool. The wall can be made from any household cardboard carton such as a tissues box. The Humptys are easy to make from table tennis balls and card, and they are about 5 cm (2 in.) in height excluding the legs. The game should be played on a table placed against a wall so that the balls can easily be retrieved after throwing.

Materials required

Three table tennis balls

Scraps of fabrics, green fur fabric or felt, paper or paint, ribbon and thin card (or thin cardboard)

A few guipure flowers

An empty cardboard carton

Small ball of knitting wool

Coloured marker pens or pencils

Adhesive

To make the wall

Use a household package such as a tissues box, or a washing powder, cereal or shoe box. If necessary, cut a hole in the back of the package as shown in the diagram so that a heavy object can be placed inside to weight it when playing the game.

Now cover the wall with paper or paint it. Glue a strip of green fur fabric or felt round the lower edge of the wall cutting the upper edge irregularly as shown in the illustration. Glue a few guipure (lace) flowers to the fur fabric or felt.

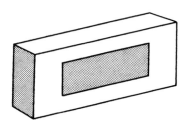

Diagram showing how to cut a hole in the back of the package

To make each Humpty Dumpty

Cut the body piece from thin card. Glue the card to the wrong side of a piece of fabric or paper then cut out 5 mm (¼ in.) larger all round. Turn and stick this extra fabric to the other side of the card. Alternatively the body can be painted. Overlap the short edges of the body 5 mm (¼ in.) and glue. Stick (i.e. glue) the table tennis ball on top of the body.

Cut one pair of arms and legs from thin white card. Colour the arms and legs as far as the feet and hands to match the body colour then mark on black stripes as shown in the illustration. Colour the feet black also.

Bend back the tops of the arms at the dotted lines and stick this portion of each arm to each side of the body close to the top. Bend up the tops of the legs at the dotted lines and stick these portions inside the front of the body. Bend up the feet then bend the legs into curves at the knees.

Mark on and colour the face using the illustration as a guide. For the hair wind a strand of wool a few times around two fingers. Tie a length of wool round the centre of the strands then stick the bunch of wool to the top of the head spacing out the wool loops evenly all round. Glue a small knot of ribbon to the front of the body.

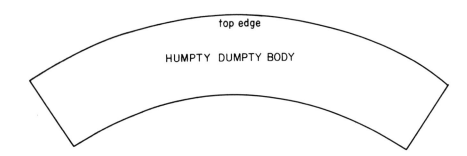

top edge

HUMPTY DUMPTY BODY

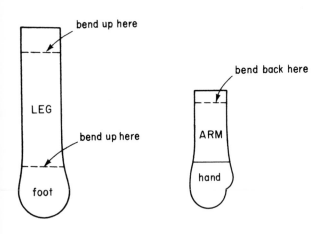

To make the throwing balls

Wind three balls of wool, each measuring about 2 cm (¾ in.) in diameter. Sew the end of the wool into each ball. Use another strand of wool to sew the wound wool strands in place here and there on the ball to make it quite firm and prevent it from unravelling.

Hansel, Gretel and the wicked witch

Hansel and Gretel are 16 cm (6¼ in.) in height and the witch measures 26 cm (10 in.). The witch's skirt has a circular cardboard base and is filled with stuffing so that she stands upright. Her blouse and the two children are all constructed from fabric rosettes threaded onto elastic. The heads and hands are made from cuttings off nylon stockings or tights, and these should be about 20 or 30 denier.

Make the fabric rosettes as explained in the instructions at the beginning of the book.

Materials required

For the heads and hands, cuttings off nylon stockings or tights and a little stuffing

Small pieces of fabrics for the rosettes, Gretel's skirt and the witch's skirt and apron

Small amounts of thin knitting wool for the hair

Scraps of black felt for the eyes, shoes and the witch's hat .

Scrap of red felt for the witch's nose

Card (thin cardboard) for the base of the witch

Red and black thread, and red and green pencils, for the facial features

Thin round elastic, 1.7 m (2 yd) in length

Adhesive

To make the witch

Cut out and gather fabric circles of the following diameters: two 9 cm (3½ in.), six 12 cm (4¾ in.) and twenty-eight 8 cm (3⅛ in.).

For the head cut a 6 cm (2¼ in.) long section from the leg portion of the nylon stocking or tights. Bring the 6 cm (2¼ in.) edges together and join them to form a tube taking a 1 cm (⅜ in.) seam. Trim the seam, then run a gathering thread round one end of the tube. Pull up the gathers tightly and finish off the thread. Turn the head right side out and stuff to form an egg-shape measuring about 16 cm (6¼ in.) around. Run a gathering thread round, 1 cm (⅜ in.) away from the remaining raw edges.

For the body cut a 30 cm (12 in.) length of elastic and fold it in half. Knot the folded end and push it inside the head. Pull up the gathers, turning the raw edges of the nylon fabric to the inside of the head. Finish off the thread, oversewing securely through the elastic.

Cut two tiny circles of black felt for the eyes then cut the nose from red felt. Glue the nose to the centre of the face then stick the eyes close together above the nose. Work black stitches for the eyebrows and mouth as shown in the illustration. For the hair sew strands of wool round the top of the head to hang down the sides and back of the head. Colour the cheeks with the moistened tip of a green pencil.

Cut the hat brim and the hat crown from black felt. Join the centre back edges of the crown piece by oversewing them together. Turn the crown right side out then oversew the lower edge to the inner edge of the brim. Place the hat on the witch's head and catch it to the head all round through the lower edge of the crown.

Now thread onto the body elastics two 9 cm (3½ in.) and one 12 cm (4¾ in.) circle. Cut a 30 cm (12 in.) length of elastic for the arms and slip this between the body elastics. Thread the remaining 12 cm (4¾ in.) circles onto the body elastics then knot the elastics together just below the circles.

For the skirt cut an 18 cm by 40 cm (7 in. by 15¾ in.) strip of fabric. Join the 18 cm (7 in.) edges taking a 1 cm (⅜ in.) seam. Turn the skirt right side out. For the base of the skirt cut a 12 cm (4¾ in.) diameter circle of card. Slip this inside one raw edge of the skirt then turn and stick this raw edge about 1 cm (⅜ in.) onto the card all round. Stuff the skirt very firmly at the base, then more lightly towards the top.

For the apron cut a 12 cm (4¾ in.) square of fabric. Fray out three of the edges a little. Tack the unfrayed edge in place having it even with the top raw edge of the skirt. Now run a gathering thread all round the top raw edge of the skirt. Pull up the gathers tightly, enclosing the knot in the body elastic, then finish off, oversewing securely through the elastic.

Onto each arm elastic, thread fourteen 8 cm (3⅛ in.) circles then knot the ends of the elastic, trimming off any excess length. For each hand cut a 3 cm by 4 cm (1¼ in. by 1⅝ in.) piece from double thickness nylon stocking fabric having the 'most stretch' in the fabric going across the 3 cm (1¼ in.) measurement. Fold the piece, bringing the 4 cm (1⅝ in.) edges together, then stitch all round close to the edges leaving one 3 cm (1¼ in.) edge open and rounding off the remaining corners. Trim the corners and turn right side out. Stuff the hands, then run a gathering thread round each one 1 cm (⅜ in.) from the raw edges. Pull up the gathers, turning the raw edges inside the hands and enclosing the knots in the arm elastics. Finish off, oversewing securely through the elastic.

To make Hansel

Cut out and gather fabric circles of the following diameters: for the bodice two 8 cm (3⅛ in.) and four 10 cm (4 in.), for each sleeve eleven 6 cm (2⅜ in.), for the trouser top three 10 cm (4 in.) and for each trouser leg fourteen 7 cm (2¾ in.)

For the head cut a 5 cm (2 in.) long section from the leg portion of the nylon stocking or tights. Bring the 5 cm (2 in.) edges together and join them, taking a 1.5 cm (½ in.) seam to form a tube. Trim the seam, then run a gathering thread round one end of the tube. Pull up the gathers tightly and finish off the thread. Turn right side out and stuff to make a ball-shape measuring about 14 cm (5½ in.) around. Run a gathering thread round 1 cm (⅜ in.) away from the remaining raw edges.

For the body cut a 30 cm (12 in.) length of elastic and fold it in half. Knot the folded end and push it inside the head. Pull up the gathers turning the raw edges of the fabric inside the head. Finish off the thread oversewing securely through the elastic.

Now thread onto the body elastics two 8 cm (3⅛

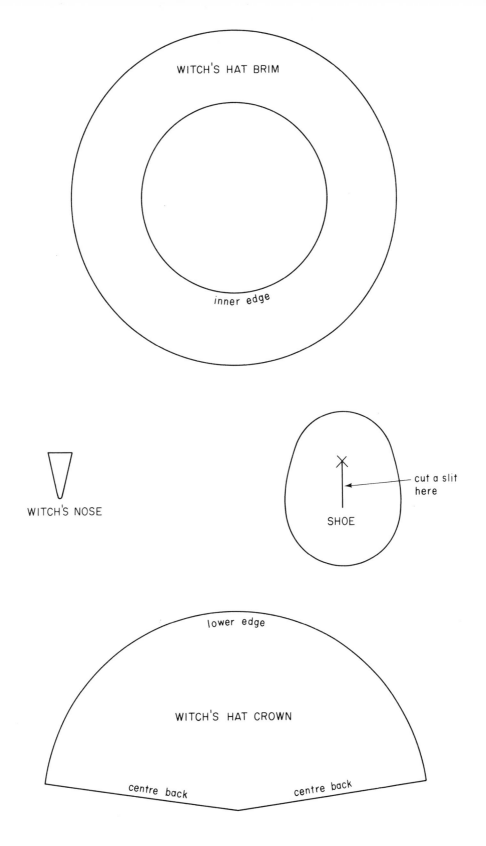

WITCH'S HAT BRIM

inner edge

WITCH'S NOSE

cut a slit here

SHOE

lower edge

WITCH'S HAT CROWN

centre back   centre back

in.) and one 10 cm (4 in.) circle. Slip a 22 cm (8¾ in.) length of elastic between the body elastics for the arms. Thread the remaining three 10 cm (4 in.) bodice circles onto the body elastics then the three 10 cm (4 in.) trouser top circles. Thread fourteen 7 cm (2¾ in.) circles onto each of the body elastics for the trouser legs then knot the ends of the elastics trimming off any excess length.

Cut four shoe pieces from felt, and cut a slit in two of the pieces for the shoe uppers as shown on the pattern. Oversew the shoe pieces together in pairs all round the edges. Stuff the shoes lightly through the slits, then push the knotted ends of the leg elastics inside the slits at the position of the cross shown on the pattern. Oversew the slit edges together catching the elastic securely in the stitching.

Onto each arm elastic, thread eleven 6 cm (2⅜ in.) circles, then knot the ends of the elastic trimming off any excess length. Make the hands and sew them in place as for the witch, using 3 cm (1¼ in.) squares of double thickness nylon stocking fabric.

Cut tiny ovals of black felt for the eyes and glue them in place half way down the face and 1 cm (⅜ in.) apart. Work a small red stitch for the mouth 1 cm (⅜ in.) below the eyes then work small black stitches for the eyelashes.

For the hair cut about eight 15 cm (6 in.) lengths of wool. Fold them in half and sew the folded ends to the centre top of the head letting the wool strands fall down the back of the head. Sew the strands to the head above the neck keeping them taut and spreading them out evenly. Continue sewing on bunches of wool in this way working towards the forehead and sides of the face until the head is completely covered with hair. Now trim all the wool strands to an even length just below the sewing line above the neck.

To make Gretel
Make all the circles and the head as for Hansel. For the skirt cut an 8 cm by 28 cm (3¼ in. by 11 in.) strip of fabric. Join the 8 cm (3¼ in.) edges taking a small seam, then make a narrow hem on one remaining raw edge. Run a gathering thread round the remaining raw edge, pull up the gathers tightly and finish off. Thread the skirt onto the body elastics between the bodice and pants top circles.

Make the hands, shoes and face as for Hansel. For Gretel's hair cut a few 20 cm (8 in.) lengths of wool and back stitch the centre of the strands to the centre parting, beginning at the forehead. Continue sewing on lengths of wool in this way to cover the head as far as the back neck. Gather the wool strands in a bunch at each side of the head and sew them there, then trim the ends to even lengths.

Playful ponies

These little toys are easy to make and no complicated patterns or gussets are required for constructing the various poses. The same four basic pattern pieces are used for each pony and they are all sewn by the stitch-around method. The ponies are first of all stitched and stuffed, then the legs are bent into various positions and caught in place against the body with a few stitches.

The standing pony measures 9 cm (3 in.) from head to tail and is about 12 cm (4¾ in.) high to the tips of his ears. Make all the pieces before assembling them in the required pose. After assembly, use the point of a needle to pick out the fleecy pile on the fabric along the seams and neck joins.

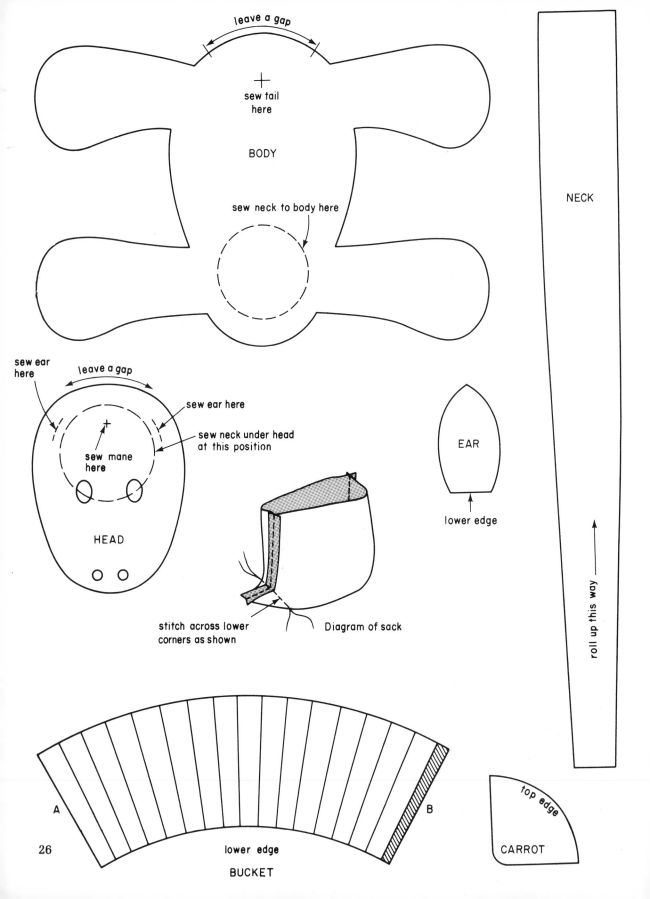

leave a gap

sew tail here

BODY

sew neck to body here

NECK

sew ear here

leave a gap

sew ear here

sew neck under head at this position

sew mane here

HEAD

EAR

lower edge

stitch across lower corners as shown

Diagram of sack

roll up this way

top edge

CARROT

A

B

26

lower edge

BUCKET

Materials required

Small pieces of fawn fleecy fabric for each pony (or 15 cm (6 in.) of this fabric 126 cm (50 in.) in width will make three ponies)

Small amount of stuffing, fawn 4 ply knitting wool, scraps of black, fawn and pink felt and black marker pen

For making the accessories, scraps of fabric, card, natural raffia, green wool, orange felt, guipure (lace) flowers and plastic-covered wire

Adhesive

To make the basic pieces

Trace the body, head, ear and neck patterns off the page onto thin paper. Pin the body pattern onto two layers of fleece having the right sides of the fabric together. Stitch all round close to the edge of the pattern leaving a gap in the seam as shown on the pattern. Cut out the body about 3 mm (⅛ in.) away from the stitching line, then remove the pattern. Turn the body right side out using the knob end of a thin knitting needle to turn each leg. Stuff the legs and the body then ladder stitch the opening. Stitch,

turn and stuff the head in the same way as for the body.

For each ear, pin the ear pattern onto a piece of felt and a piece of fleece, having the right sides of the fabric together. Trim the fabrics even with the lower edge of the pattern. Stitch round the ear close to the edge of the pattern leaving the lower edges open. Remove the pattern, cut out the ear close to the stitching line, then turn right side out. Fold the ear in half at the lower edge, then oversew all the edges together.

Cut the neck strip from fleecy fabric. Beginning at the narrow end, closely roll up the strip along the length then oversew the wide end in place. The neck should now measure about 2.5 cm (1 in.) in diameter.

To assemble the pieces

Assemble the pieces as follows but also refer to the instructions for each of the individual ponies.

Decide on which pose is required, then bend and pin the legs in the appropriate positions. Catch the legs in place with a few secure stitches where they

The leaping pony

touch the body or each other. Now pin the neck on top of the body at the position shown on the pattern, then slip stitch it in place. Pin, then stitch the head on top of the neck at the position shown on the head pattern, turning the head to one side if the pose requires it. Pin, then sew the lower edges of the ears to the head at the positions shown on the head pattern.

For the mane, wind a strand of wool twenty-five times around three fingers. Tie a strand of wool round the centre of this small hank and sew this tied centre to the position shown on the head pattern. Make another mane piece in the same way and sew it to the head behind the first piece. Catch the wool loops to the head, forehead and neck with a stitch or two here and there to hold them in place.

For the tail, wind the wool round the fingers as for the mane then cut once through the strands. Tie a strand of wool round the centre of the lengths of wool then trim the ends of the wool to taper the end of the tail slightly. Sew the centre of the tail to the position shown on the body pattern.

For the nostrils cut tiny circles of pink felt, using a leather punch to cut these if one is available. Mark the centre of each circle with a black dot then stick the nostrils in place. For the wide-open eyes cut ovals of black felt as shown on the head pattern and stick in place. For the half-closed eyes cut ovals of black felt then onto these glue half ovals of pink felt. For the sleeping eyes cut ovals of pink felt, trim a little off the lower edges then mark along this edge with black pen.

To make the leaping pony
Sew the legs in place, stretching them right out at the back and front. For the log cut a strip of card and roll it up to make a tube measuring about 2.5 cm (1 in.) in diameter by 8 cm (3 in.) in length. Cut two 2.5 cm (1 in.) diameter circles of card and mark them with tree growing rings, then stick one to each end of the log. Cover the log by gluing round a strip of brown felt or fabric. Glue a few bits of green wool to the log for grass, then stick on a few guipure (lace) flowers.

To make the sleeping pony
Pull one back leg across underneath the body, squashing it to lie as flat as possible, then sew it in

The sleeping pony

(Above) the muching pony, (below) the standing pony

The pony with carrots

place. Sew the other legs in the positions illustrated. Lower the head a little and catch it to the neck about half way down.

For the sack cut a 10 cm by 20 cm (4 in. by 8 in.) strip of fabric. Fold the strip, bringing the 10 cm (4 in.) edges together, then take a tiny seam down each side. Stitch across the lower corners of the sack as shown in the diagram then turn the sack right side out. Turn in the top raw edges 1 cm (⅜ in.) and stick down. Put a little stuffing in the sack and tie a thread round the top as illustrated.

To make the munching pony
Place the back legs along either side of the body and the front legs in an almost upright position, then sew them in place.

Cut the bucket from thin card. Colour it brown, then mark on the lines as shown on the pattern. Lap the edge marked A over the shaded portion of the edge marked B and stick in place. Cut a circle of card to fit the bottom of the bucket and glue it in place. For the black bands around the bucket, cut 3 mm (⅛ in.) wide strips of card coloured black, and glue them around the bucket as illustrated. Use a

length of plastic-covered wire for the bucket handle fixing it into the bucket at each side below the top band.

Glue bits of raffia inside the bucket for straw. Sew a few strands of raffia through the pony's head at the front below the seam line using a dab of adhesive to hold them in place.

To make the standing pony
Pin and sew the legs straight down onto the body as shown in the illustration.

To make the pony with carrots
Pin the back legs in a standing position and stretch the front legs almost flat out in front. Sew in place. Make the carrot sack in the same way as for the sleeping pony, using a 7 cm by 14 cm (2¾ in. by 5½ in.) strip of fabric. Roll down the top of the sack.

Cut the carrots from orange felt using the pattern. Stick on a few strands of green wool so that they will protrude at the top edge. Roll up each carrot to form a cone-shape, then sew the edge in place. Gather round the top edges and finish off.

Lavender dolls

The dolls are 10 cm (4 in.) in height and their bodies are filled with dried lavender flowers. They are designed so that the flowers can be renewed as necessary, through a small hole in the base.

Materials required for one doll

An 18 mm (¾ in.) diameter white or fawn bead for the head

Dried lavender flowers

Thin fabric such as net curtaining for the body

Scraps of coloured fabric, card (thin cardboard), felt, ribbon, trimmings, clear adhesive tape, nylon stocking fabric and feathers

Black marker pen and red pencil

Adhesive

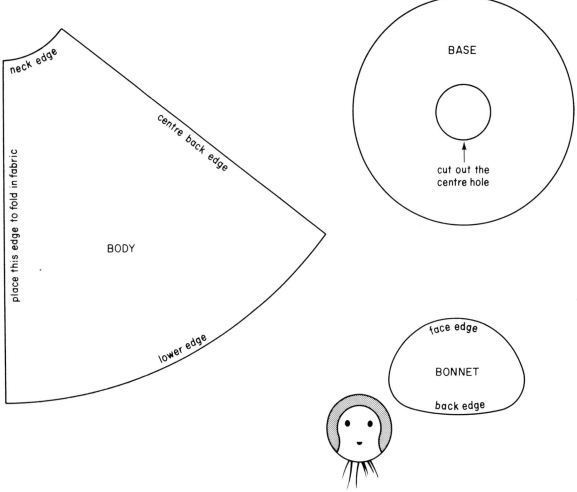

Diagram showing how to
mark on the features

To make the doll

Cut out the body piece placing the edge indicated on the pattern to a fold in the net fabric. Join the centre back edges taking a tiny seam. Turn the body right side out.

To cover the bead cut a small piece of nylon stocking fabric and pull it over the bead gathering all the edges tightly together. Tie a thread round the gathers securing the bead inside the fabric. Trim off the stocking fabric about 1 cm (⅜ in.) away from the tied thread.

Run a gathering thread round the neck edge of the body, push the raw edges of the stocking fabric right inside the neck edge of the body then pull up the gathers tightly and finish off, oversewing the fabrics together.

Cut the base from card, then cut out the centre hole. Place the base inside the lower edge of the body, then stick the lower edge of the body fabric about 1 cm (⅜ in.) onto the base all round.

Now fill the body with lavender flowers through the hole in the base, packing it in very tightly so that the body is quite firm. Place a piece of clear adhesive tape over the hole in the base.

Mark on the hair and eyes with black marker pen and also colour the mouth and cheeks with red pencil using the diagram as a guide. Stick a bit of lace trimming round the neck and across the top of the head as shown in the illustration. Glue lace and trimming round the lower edge of the body also.

Cut the bonnet from felt and stick it across the back of the head, then glue a few feathers and trimming to one side.

For the shawl cut a 10 cm (4 in.) square of fabric and fray out all the raw edges a little. Fold the shawl and stick it in position round the doll as illustrated then glue a tiny ribbon bow to the front.

Three bears cottage

The cottage is a plump little stuffed cushion measuring 28 cm (11 in.) in length and standing 23 cm (9 in.) high. The three bears, 13 cm (5 in.) high, live in the door and window pockets, one for each bear.

Seams of 1 cm (⅜ in.) are allowed on the cottage wall pieces. Seams of 5 mm (¼ in.) are allowed on the bear patterns and all the cottage door and window pieces.

Materials required

For the cottage walls, 40 cm (½ yd) of 91 cm (36 in.) wide plain fabric

For the windows, door and roof etc, oddments of fabrics, green fur fabric, braid and felt

Permanent black marker pen for marking the stones on the walls

For the bears, scraps of fleecy fabric, black thread and small beads or felt for the eyes

Strong card (cardboard), for the base of the cottage 500 g (1 lb) of stuffing

To make the cottage

Cut two 34 cm by 40 cm (13½ in. by 15¾ in.) pieces of fabric for the walls. For the roof cut two 12 cm by 40 cm (4¾ in. by 15¾ in.) strips of fabric. Fray out each roof strip a little along one long edge. Place a roof strip on the right side of each wall piece as shown in diagram 1. Cut the sloping sides of the roof off both the roof and wall pieces as shown in the diagram. Sew the roof strips in place all round the edges.

Now join the cottage wall pieces together all round the edges, leaving a 13 cm (5 in.) gap in the seam at the top of the roof. To make the flat base of the cottage, bring the lower seam and the side seam together at each lower corner, pressing both seams open. Now stitch across each corner at right angles to it, and 6 cm (2½ in.) away from the corner point, as shown in diagram 2. Trim off these corners and turn the cottage right side out.

For the base cut a 12 cm by 26 cm (4¾ in. by 10¼ in.) strip of strong card. Round off the corners of the card then slip it inside the cottage placing it flat against the base. Stuff the cottage firmly then slip stitch the opening in the roof.

For the cottage doorway cut a 10 cm by 14 cm (4 in. by 5½ in.) strip of black felt. Sew the doorway in place on the cottage wall, having the left side of it about 9 cm (3½ in.) away from the side seam of the cottage, and the lower edge even with the base.

For the lower half of the door, which is a pocket, cut a 12 cm by 18 cm (4¾ in. by 7 in.) strip of fabric. Fold the strip bringing the 12 cm (4¾ in.) edges together. Join all the raw edges leaving a gap for turning. Turn right side out, press, then slip stitch the gap. Note that the widest measurement of the piece is the width of the door. If desired, work lines of stitching on the piece as illustrated for a wood panelled effect. Sew the lower door piece to the doorway at the lower and side edges, easing the lower edge to fit the lower edge of the doorway.

Cut two upper door pieces using the pattern. Join the pieces round the edges leaving a gap for turning. Turn, press and slip stitch the gap. Sew the narrow side of the upper door to the left hand side of the doorway as illustrated. Sew a strip of braid all round the edge of the doorway.

For the window frame cut an 11 cm by 14 cm (4¼ in. by 5½ in.) strip of fabric. Fold the strip bringing the 11 cm (4¼ in.) edges together and make as for the lower door piece. For the window, sew a piece of black felt to the frame cutting it 1 cm (⅜ in.) smaller all round. Sew on small pieces of fabric for the curtains at each side of the window as illustrated turning in the raw edges of the fabric to neaten.

Sew the window to the wall beside the door as illustrated placing the lower edge about 7 cm (2¾ in.) up from the base of the cottage. For the lower pocket beneath the window use a piece of fabric to match the walls. Make the pocket in exactly the same way as for the lower door. Sew a strip of the same fabric as the window frame to the top edge of

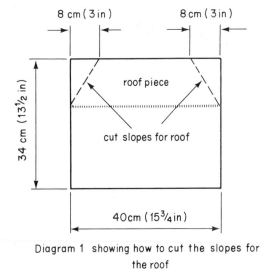

Diagram 1 showing how to cut the slopes for the roof

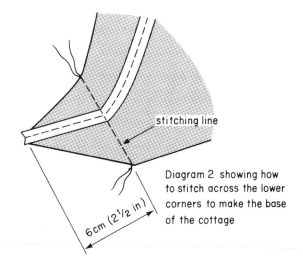

Diagram 2 showing how to stitch across the lower corners to make the base of the cottage

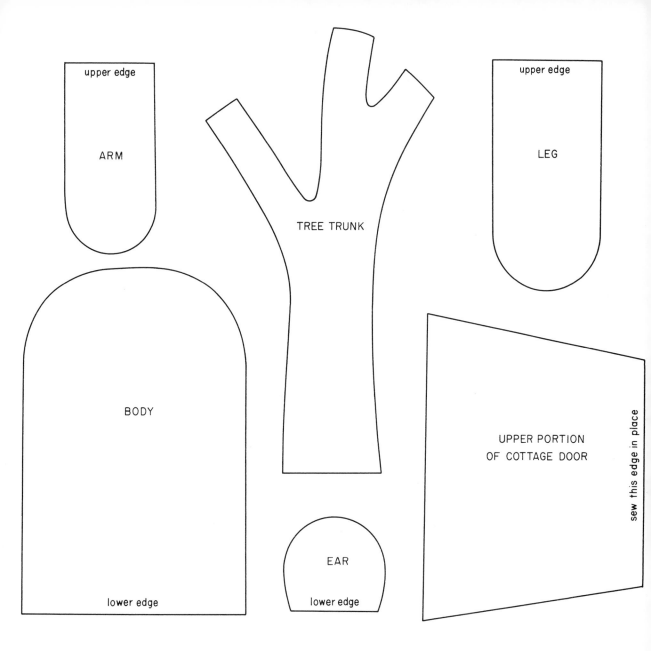

the pocket for the window sill. Now sew the pocket in place beneath the window in the same way as for the lower door piece.

Make another window in exactly the same way and sew it to the back wall of the cottage as illustrated. Cut the tree trunk from brown felt and sew it in place beside the window. Cut irregular shapes from green fur fabric for the foliage and sew them to the tree as illustrated. Cut narrow strips of green fur fabric and sew to the cottage walls at the base

all round except for the cottage door.

For the sign on the cottage roof, cut a 5 cm by 8 cm (2 in. by 3¼ in.) piece of fabric. Turn in all the raw edges 5 mm (¼ in.) and tack, then turn in the corners. Onto this piece, sew an oval of fabric with the words printed in marker pen as illustrated. Sew the sign in place on the roof.

Use black pen to mark the stones on the cottage walls here and there, then shade the stones lightly with pencil.

Back view of the cottage

To make a bear

Cut two body pieces from fleecy fabric and join them round the edges leaving the lower edges open. Turn right side out and stuff lightly then turn in the raw edges and slip stitch them together. Tie a thread tightly round the body 5 cm (2 in.) down from the top seam, to form the neck.

Make the arms and legs as for the body then sew them to the body as illustrated. Cut four ear pieces and join them in pairs leaving the lower edges open. Turn them right side out, then turn in and slip stitch the raw edges pulling the stitches to gather slightly. Sew the ears to the head seam, placing them about 1 cm (⅜ in.) apart.

Position the eyes on the head half way down the face and 2.5 cm (1 in. apart, using beads, or circles of felt if the toy is for a very young child. Sew on the eyes taking stitches through the front of the face from one eye to the other. Pull up the stitches slightly and finish off. Use black thread to work a tiny triangle for the nose between the eyes, then work an inverted Y-shape below this for the mouth.

Little boy blue
and little girl pink

These cuddly twin rag dolls are very easy to make from a simple one-piece pattern using the stitch-around method. They are about 30 cm (12 in.) in height and their clothes can be removed except for the hats and shoes which are sewn in place. Since the body pattern is too large to fit on the page it is printed in two pieces. These should be traced off the page and joined with clear adhesive tape as given in the instructions.

The shoes and boy's cap peak are made by the stitch-around method and all other seam allowances are given in the instructions.

(Left) little girl pink, (right) little boy blue

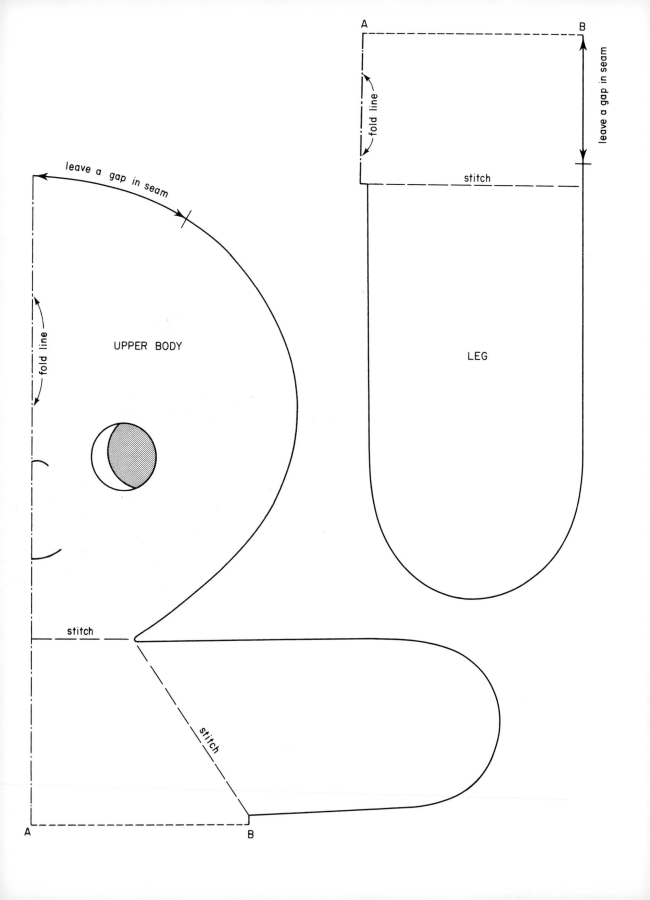

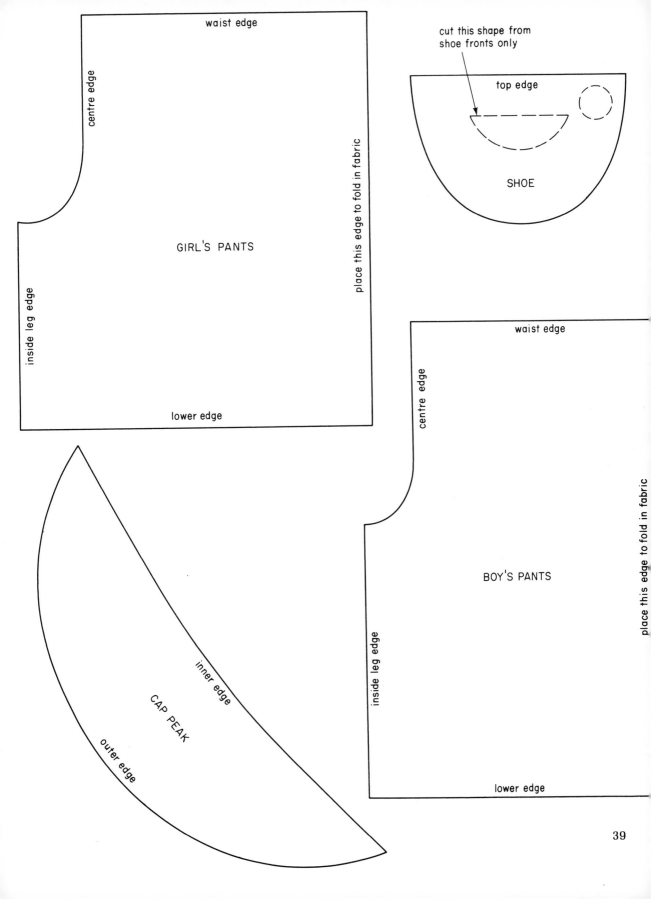

waist edge

centre edge

inside leg edge

place this edge to fold in fabric

GIRL'S PANTS

lower edge

cut this shape from shoe fronts only

top edge

SHOE

waist edge

centre edge

place this edge to fold in fabric

BOY'S PANTS

inside leg edge

lower edge

inner edge

outer edge

CAP PEAK

39

Materials required for the two dolls

For the dolls, 50 cm (20 in.) of 91 cm (36 in.) wide
   white cotton fabric
Scraps of black and blue felt, red thread, red ball-
   point pen and red pencil, for the facial features
Small pieces of felt for the shoes
Ball of chunky knitting wool, 25 g (1 oz), and 70 cm
   (¾ yd) of narrow tape or ribbon, for the hair
About 125 g (¼ lb) of stuffing
Small pieces of ribbon, lace edging, trimming and
   narrow elastic or shirring elastic
Oddments of fabrics for the clothes
Adhesive

To make the full size body pattern

Fold two pieces of tracing or thin paper, then place
the folds along the dotted lines marked 'fold line' on
the upper body and leg patterns. Trace off the
patterns, then cut them out, keeping the paper
folded. Open up the folded patterns and join them
together with clear adhesive (Scotch) tape at the
edge marked A-B.

To make the basic doll

Pin the body pattern onto two layers of white
cotton fabric, placing the pins about 1 cm (⅜ in.)
inside the edges of the pattern. Stitch all round
close to the edge of the pattern leaving gaps in the
stitching at the top of the head and one side of the
body, as indicated on the pattern. Remove the
pattern and cut the fabric between the doll's legs.
Cut out the doll about 5 mm (¼ in.) away from the
stitching line. Turn the doll right side out and stitch
across the neck through both thicknesses of fabric
as shown on the pattern.

Stuff the head firmly, then slip stitch the opening.
Stuff the arms, then stitch from the underarms to
the neck through both thicknesses of fabric as
shown on the pattern. Next stuff the legs, and then
stitch across the tops as shown on the pattern.
Finally, stuff the body and slip stitch the opening.

Mark the mouth and nose lightly on the face with
red pen. Work the mouth in red stitches then work
back along the line, oversewing through each
stitch. Cut circles of blue felt for the eyes, then cut
the shaded portions of the eyes from black felt and
glue these to the blue felt circles as shown on the
pattern. Place the eyes in position on the doll, but
before gluing them in place, colour the cheeks with
the moistened tip of the red pencil. Glue the eyes in
place.

For the hair cut a 34 cm (13½ in.) length of tape or
ribbon, and place one end under the sewing machine
foot. Wind the chunky wool straight off the ball,

three times round three fingers of the left hand. Slip
these loops off the hand and stitch one end of the
loops to the tape. Continue making and sewing on
loops in this way until the length of tape is covered.
Pin this looped fringe across the top of the doll's
forehead then round towards the back of the head
above the neck. When making the girl doll, pin the
hair a little lower down than the boy's at the back.
Sew the hair to the head through the stitching line
on the tape.

To make the shoes

Pin the shoe pattern onto two layers of felt, then
trim the felt even with the pattern at the top edge.
Stitch all round the curved edge close to the pattern.
Remove the pattern and cut out the shoe close to the
stitching line. Cut out the shape shown on the pattern for the fronts of the shoes. Place the shoes on
the doll and slip stitch the top edges to the legs. Cut
two small circles of felt for buttons and stick these
to the sides of the shoes as illustrated.

To make the girl's pants

Cut two pants pieces, placing the edge indicated on
the pattern to a fold in the fabric. Turn in the lower
edge of each piece 1 cm (⅜ in.) and press. Turn in the
raw edges of these turnings and stitch down, form-

ing the casings for the elastic. Sew lace trimmings to the lower edges then thread elastic through the casings to fit the legs, holding it in place at each end with a stitch or two.

Join the pants pieces together at the centre edges, taking 5 mm (¼ in.) seams. Clip the curves in the seams. Bring these centre seams together and join the inside leg edges, taking 5 mm (¼ in.) seams. Turn in and hem the waist edge in the same way as for the lower edges, then thread through elastic to fit the waist.

To make the girl's dress
Cut two 11 cm by 18 cm (4¼ in. by 7 in.) strips of fabric. Join the pieces together at the short edges for 3 cm (1¼ in.) only, taking a 1 cm (⅜ in.) seam. Turn in the remainder of these short raw edges 1 cm (⅜ in.) and stitch down, forming the armhole edges of the dress. Hem the lower edge of the dress as for the lower edge of the pants and then sew on lace trimming.

Hem the remaining edges for the neck edges in the same way. Thread elastic round through both neck edges to fit the neck and knot the ends of the elastic together. Sew a ribbon bow to the neck edge at the front. The dress should be put on or removed by taking it over the doll's legs.

To make the girl's hat
Cut two 34 cm (13½ in.) diameter circles of fabric. Join them round the edges taking a 5 mm (¼ in.) seam and leaving a gap in the seam for turning. Turn the hat right side out and press, but do not sew the gap in the seam at this stage. Lightly mark a line all round or use pins, 6 cm (2¼ in.) from the edge of the hat. Stitch all round this line, then stitch all round again 5 mm (¼ in.) outside the first stitching line, leaving a small gap in the stitching. Thread elastic between the stitching lines taking the elastic through the gap left in the outside seam. Pull up the elastic so that the hat fits on the doll's head, then join the ends. Finish off the line of stitching then slip stitch the gap in the outside seam.

Stuff the crown of the hat lightly to make it a nice rounded shape then place the hat on the head having the elastic on top of the stitching line on the hair. Sew the hat to the head all round at this position, using a large needle, and taking small stitches through the hat and large stitches into the head.

To make the boy's pants
Make the boy's pants in the same basic way as for the girl's, using the boy's pants pattern. Omit the elastic at the lower and waist edges and also the lace trimming.

To make the boy's smock
Cut out and make as for the girl's dress but sew ric-rac or other trimming to the hem edge instead of lace. Sew a large ribbon bow to the neck edge at the centre front.

To make the boy's cap
For the cap band cut a 2 cm by 35 cm (¾ in. by 13¾ in.) strip of stiff fabric or interfacing. Cut a 4 cm by 35 cm (1½ in. by 13¾ in.) strip of the cap fabric. Glue the narrow strip centrally on the wrong side of the cap fabric strip. Turn and glue the long edges of the fabric strip to the other side of the narrow strip. Now join the short edges of the cap band taking a 5 mm (¼ in.) seam.

For the crown of the cap cut a 30 cm (12 in.) diameter circle of fabric. Gather round the circle 1 cm (⅜ in.) inside the raw edge and pull up the gathers to fit inside the cap band. Slip this gathered edge 1 cm (⅜ in.) inside one edge of the cap band having the right sides of both outside. Pin it in place spacing out the gathers evenly all round. Stitch all round through the edge of the band so that the gathered crown is held in place.

Pin the cap peak pattern onto two layers of fabric

having the right sides of the fabric together. Trim the fabric even with the inner edge of the pattern. Stitch round the outer edge close to the pattern. Remove the pattern and cut out the peak close to the stitching line. Turn right side out and press. Now cut one peak piece from stiff fabric or interfacing making it slightly smaller than the pattern. Slip this inside the cap peak between the layers of fabric then stitch round the edge of the peak through all thicknesses.

Slip the inner raw edges of the cap peak 1 cm (⅜ in.) inside the lower edge of the cap band having the right sides of both outside. Pin the peak in place. Now stitch all round the lower edge of the band through all thicknesses catching the peak in place.

Stuff the crown of the cap lightly, then spread adhesive all round the inside of the cap band. Place the cap on the head having the lower edge of the band on the hair stitching line. Hold the band in position with pins until the adhesive is dry. Pull the crown over to one side and catch it to the band where it touches with a few stitches. Sew a small ribbon bow to the other side of the band as illustrated.

The owl and the pussy cat

The owl and the pussy cat soft toys, each 10 cm (4 in.) high, can be popped into their pea-green boat in the picture, or made as amusing egg cosies for keeping boiled eggs warm at the table.

The picture is easy to make from a piece of card cut off a grocery box, and only scraps of felt and fabrics are required for the toys. Seams of 3 mm (⅛ in.) are allowed on all pieces unless otherwise stated.

Materials required for the egg cosies
Small pieces of felt and printed fabrics
Scraps of ribbon and trimmings
Sequins for the centres of the eyes
Black thread
Adhesive

To make the egg cosies
For the owl, cut two body pieces and two ears from

felt. Pin the lower edges of the ears at the top of one of the body pieces having them 4 cm (1½ in.) apart and the curved edges of body and ears even. Place the other body piece on top of the first piece and stitch all round, leaving the lower edges open and catching the ears in the seam. Turn the body right side out.

From printed fabric cut a 5.5 cm by 19 cm (2¼ in. by 7½ in.) strip. Turn in the long edges 3 mm (⅛ in.) and stitch, then join the short edges of the strip. Turn right side out and slip over the owl, having the upper edge even with the dotted line shown on the body pattern. Slip stitch this edge of the strip and the lower edge in place.

Cut four wing pieces and join them in pairs by stitching 3 mm (⅛ in.) from the edges, leaving the upper edges open. Sew the top of each wing to the owl as illustrated, 3 mm (⅛ in.) down from the top edge of the printed fabric. Sew a length of narrow ribbon round the owl to cover the top edges of the wings then tie it in a bow at the front.

Cut two eyes and one beak from felt. Glue the beak to the centre of the face. Work lines on the eyes using black thread as shown on the pattern, then sew a sequin to the centre of each one. Glue the eyes in position lapping the beak a little at each side.

Make the cat as for the owl placing the ears 1.5 cm (½ in.) apart. Use the arm pattern instead of the wings and sew trimming round the top edge of the printed fabric and a small bow to the head. Cut the eyes from felt and sew a sequin to the centre of each before gluing in place. Work the nose, mouth and whiskers in black thread as shown on the body pattern.

Materials required for the soft toys
As for the egg cosies plus a little stuffing

To make the toys
Make in same way as for the egg cosies, putting a little stuffing in the wings and arms before sewing them in place. Sew the owl's wings to the positions shown on the body pattern so that the guitar can be held. Cut the base piece from felt, then stuff the toy and oversew the base to the lower edge matching points A.

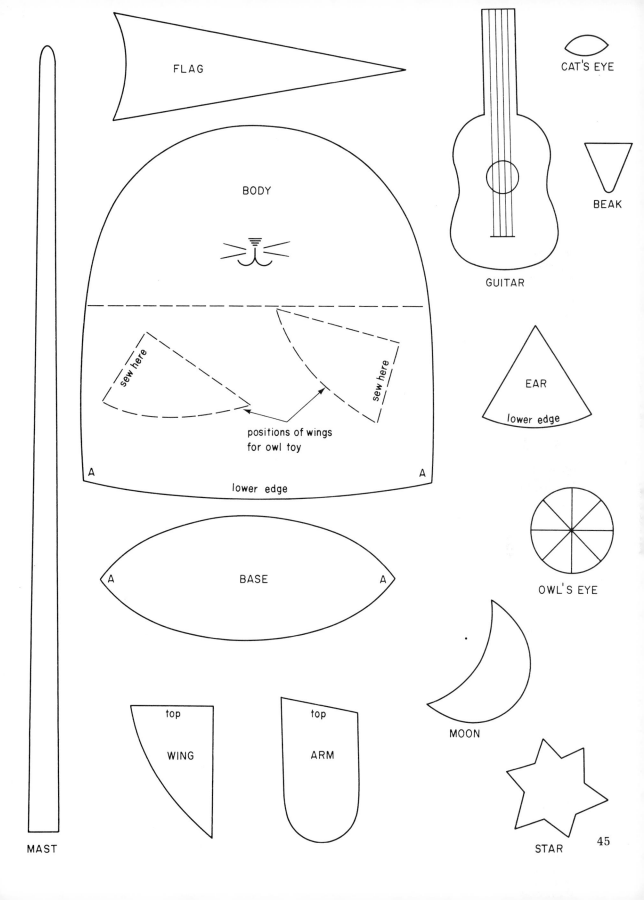

FLAG

CAT'S EYE

BODY

GUITAR

BEAK

sew here

sew here

positions of wings
for owl toy

EAR

lower edge

A   A

lower edge

OWL'S EYE

BASE

A   A

MOON

MAST

top

WING

top

ARM

STAR

45

For the guitar, glue three layers of felt together then cut it out using the pattern. Stick on a small circle of felt for the centre hole, then work the strings in black thread.

Materials required for the pocket picture

A 30 cm by 40 cm (12 in. by 16 in.) piece of cardboard cut from a grocery box

Dark blue fabric for covering both sides of the card

Light blue jumbo ric-rac braid, 1 m (1 yd) in length

Narrow white ric-rac braid, 1 m (1 yd) in length

For the boat, two 16.5 cm by 23 cm (6½ in. by 9 in.) pieces of green felt and 50 cm (½ yd) of braid

Small pieces of felt

Furnishing (finishing) braid, 2 cm (¾ in.) in width, 1.5 m (1⅝ yd) in length, for edging the picture, and a scrap of ribbon for the hanging loop

Adhesive

To make the picture

Glue on rectangles of blue fabric to cover the front and back of the card. Glue on strips of ric-rac braids for the sea, alternating the colours and placing the first strip 2.5 cm (1 in.) up from the lower edge of the picture. Stick braid round the outer edge of the picture, folding the edges onto the front and back to cover the raw edges of the fabric.

Cut the moon from yellow felt, and five stars from white felt, then glue them in place as illustrated.

For the boat, glue the two pieces of green felt together round the edges, then work lines of machine stitching across, about 1.5 cm (½ in.) apart, parallel to the 23 cm (9 in.) edges. Fold the boat, bringing the long edges together, then stitch across the short edges taking sloping seams, tapering from 5 mm (¼ in.) at the open edges to 2.5 cm (1 in.) at the folded edge. Trim the seams, and turn the boat right side out. Sew braid to one upper edge of the boat on the outside and the other upper edge on the inside so that both will be visible when the boat is stuck on the picture.

Spread adhesive on the boat at the back leaving about 2.5 cm (1 in.) unglued at each side next to the seams. Pin the boat to the picture in the position illustrated and leave until the adhesive is dry.

Cut the mast from felt and glue in position. Cut the flag from felt and glue in place in folds as though fluttering in the breeze. Glue a loop of ribbon to the back of the picture close to the top edge for hanging it up.

Five jungle animals

The jungle animals are all made from fabric rosettes threaded onto lengths of round elastic. The elephant stands 11 cm (4¼ in.) high and is 16 cm (6¼ in.) in length. The monkey, lion and tiger measure 9 cm (3½ in.) and the snake is 23 cm (9 in.) long.

Details of suitable colours of fabrics and felt for each animal are given in the individual instructions. Make the fabric rosettes as given at the beginning of the book.

Materials required

Small pieces of fabrics for the rosettes
Scraps of knitting wool, fawn fur fabric, felt, stuffing, black thread
Short lengths of thin round elastic
Black and brown permanent marker pen
Adhesive

To make the lion

For the lion use yellow or gold-coloured fabric and felt. The lion illustrated is made from gold and white gingham fabric. Cut out and gather fabric circles of the following diameters: one 5 cm (2 in.), nineteen 6 cm (2⅜ in.), three 7 cm (2¾ in.) and six 8 cm (3⅛ in.).

For the tail cut six 20 cm (8 in.) lengths of thin yellow knitting wool. Fold the lengths in half and slip a 10 cm (4 in.) length of round elastic through the folded ends of the wool, and bring the ends of the elastic together forming the body elastics. Plait the wool strands for about 6 cm (2⅜ in.), then tie a thread round the ends to hold them in place.

Now onto the double body elastic thread a 5 cm (2 in.) gathered circle and sew it securely to the tail. Thread onto the body elastics one 6 cm (2⅜ in.), one 7 cm (2¾ in.), and one 8 cm (3⅛ in.) circle, then pass a 10 cm (4 in.) length of elastic between the body elastics for the back legs. Thread onto the body elastics five 8 cm (3⅛ in.) circles then pass another 10 cm (4 in.) length of elastic between the body elastics for the front legs. Finally thread on two 7 cm (2¾ in.) and two 6 cm (2⅜ in.) circles.

For the lion's mane cut a 10 cm (4 in.) diameter circle of fur fabric, and gather it into a rosette as for the other circles. Pass the body elastics through this circle and knot them together, trimming off any excess length. Sew the knot securely to the fur fabric circle. For the lion's head cut the front head piece from felt then fold it in half and oversew the underface edges together. Turn right side out and push in some stuffing. Place the front head piece centrally over the lion's mane. Slip stitch the outer edge to the mane all round, leaving the ears free, and adding more stuffing before completing the sewing to make the head quite firm. Cut the eyes from black felt and the nose from brown felt, then stick them in place. Work the mouth in small black stitches as illustrated.

Onto each leg elastic, thread four 6 cm (2⅜ in.) circles. Knot the ends of each elastic, trimming off any excess length. For each foot cut two foot pieces from felt. Cut a slit in one of the pieces as shown on the pattern. Now oversew or whip stitch the foot pieces together round the edges, then stuff them through the slit. Push the knotted ends of the leg elastic inside the foot at the position of the cross shown on the pattern. Oversew or whip stitch the slit to close it, taking the stitches through the elastic to hold the knot in place inside the foot.

To hold the legs in an upright position so that the lion will stand up, catch the lowest leg circles together with a stitch or two where they touch.

To make the tiger

For the tiger use orange felt for the head, feet and tail, and orange and black fabrics for the gathered rosettes.

Cut the tail from felt then mark on the stripes

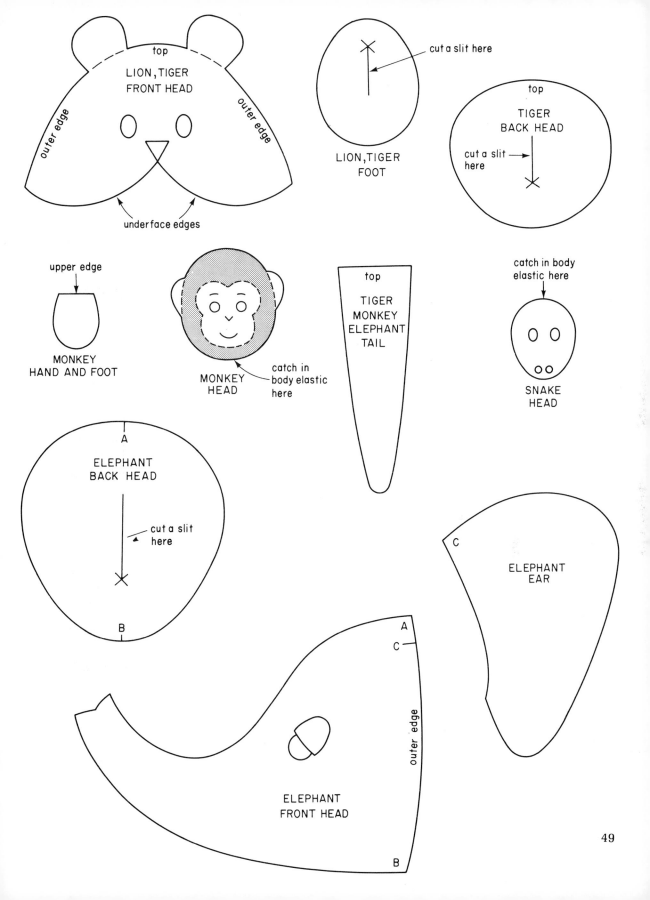

top

LION, TIGER FRONT HEAD

outer edge

outer edge

underface edges

cut a slit here

LION, TIGER FOOT

top

TIGER BACK HEAD

cut a slit here

upper edge

MONKEY HAND AND FOOT

MONKEY HEAD

catch in body elastic here

top

TIGER MONKEY ELEPHANT TAIL

catch in body elastic here

SNAKE HEAD

A

ELEPHANT BACK HEAD

cut a slit here

B

C

ELEPHANT EAR

A
C

outer edge

ELEPHANT FRONT HEAD

B

49

using a black pen. Oversew or whip stitch the long edges together. Cut a 10 cm (4 in.) length of elastic for the body, fold it in half and sew the folded end securely into the top of the tail.

Make and thread on fabric rosettes as for the lion but make them alternately black and orange for a striped effect.

Cut out and sew the front head pieces as for the lion, then cut the back head piece from felt. Cut a slit in the back head piece as shown on the pattern. Oversew the front head to the back head all round, tucking in the ears at the dotted lines so that they will be on the outside when the head is turned right side out. Turn the head right side out through the slit, then stuff it firmly. Push the knot in the body elastic inside the head at the position of the cross then oversew the slit to close it, sewing through the elastic to hold the knot in place.

Make the facial features as for the lion and mark the head with black pen as illustrated. Make the feet as for the lion.

To make the monkey

Brown and white striped fabric is used for the monkey illustrated, with light brown felt for the head, tail, feet and hands.

Cut out and gather circles of the following diameters: thirty-nine 3 cm (1⅛ in.), three 3.5 cm (1⅜ in.), six 4 cm (1⅝ in.), two 4.5 cm (1¾ in.) and two 5 cm (2 in.).

For the body cut a 16 cm (6¼ in.) length of elastic then fold it in half. Cut two head pieces from felt. Oversew them together all round the edges catching in the folded end of the body elastic at the lower edge as shown on the pattern and stuffing the head before completing the sewing. Colour the head with brown pen except for the ears and face as shown on the pattern. Cut the eyes from black felt and stick them in place, or alternatively use black pen to mark them on the face. Work the mouth, nose and eyebrows in small black stitches.

Now thread three 4 cm (1⅝ in.) circles onto the double body elastic, and pass a 10 cm (4 in.) length of elastic between the body elastics for the arms. Thread onto the body elastics one 4.5 cm (1¾ in.), two 5 cm (2 in.), and one 4.5 cm (1¾ in.) circle, then pass a 12 cm (4¾ in.) length of elastic between the body elastics for the legs. To complete the body,

thread on one 4 cm (1⅝ in.), one 3.5 cm (1⅜ in.) and one 3 cm (1⅛ in.) circle, then knot the elastics together, trimming off any excess length. Make the tail as for the tiger, push the knotted end of the elastic inside and sew it in place. Lightly mark the tail all over with brown pen.

Onto each arm elastic thread nine 3 cm (1⅛ in.) circles. Onto each leg elastic thread one 4 cm (1⅝ in.), one 3.5 cm (1⅜ in.) and ten 3 cm (1⅛ in.) circles. Knot the ends of all the elastics, trimming off any excess length. For each hand and foot cut two from felt. Oversew them together leaving the upper edges open. Push in a little stuffing, then oversew the upper edges together enclosing and sewing in the knotted end of the arm or leg elastic. Colour the hands and feet to match the tail.

To make the snake
Green and red patterned fabrics are used for the snake illustrated, having three circles of green then one of red and repeating this sequence all along the body.

Cut out and gather about forty-four 3 cm (1⅛ in.) diameter circles. For the tapered shape at the end of the body cut and gather about sixteen circles making each one slightly smaller than the one before.

For the body cut a 25 cm (10 in.) length of elastic and knot one end. Cut two head pieces from felt and oversew them together round the edges, pushing in a little stuffing, and sewing in the knotted end of the body elastic as shown on the pattern. Cut the eyes and nostrils from black felt and stick in place, or alternatively mark them on the head with black pen.

Thread all the 3 cm (1⅛ in.) circles onto the elastic, then the smaller circles for the tapered end of the body. Knot the end of the elastic and trim off any excess length. For the tail end of the body cut a 4 cm (1⅝ in.) diameter circle of fabric. Fold the circle in half, having the right side outside, then turn in the raw edges and run round a gathering thread. Wrap this semicircle of fabric round the knot in the end of the body elastic to form a cone-shape. Pull up the gathers and finish off, sewing the tail end to the elastic.

To make the elephant
Use grey fabric and felt for the elephant. The one

52

illustrated is made from grey fabric dotted with white.

Cut out and gather circles of the following diameters: forty-two 8 cm (3¼ in.), five 9 cm (3⅝ in.), five 10 cm (4 in.), two 11 cm (4⅜ in.), four 12 cm (4¾ in.) and six 14 cm (5½ in.).

To make the head cut two front head pieces from felt and oversew them together round the edges, leaving the outer edges marked A-B on the pattern open. Cut the back head piece from felt and cut a slit in it as shown on the pattern. Oversew the outer edge of the front head piece to the back head piece matching points A and B. Turn the head right side out through the slit using a thin knitting needle to turn the trunk carefully. Stuff the head firmly through the slit.

For the body cut a 30 cm (12 in.) length of elastic. Fold it in half and knot the ends together. Push the knot inside the head at the position of the cross shown on the pattern. Oversew or whip stitch the slit to close it, catching the elastic in the sewing to hold the knot securely in place.

Cut the ears from felt and sew one to each side of the head seam, matching the points marked C. Cut the eyes from black felt and the eyelids from pink felt, then stick them in place. Onto the folded end of the body elastic, thread one 11 cm (4⅜ in.), then one 12 cm (4¾ in.) circle. Pass a 20 cm (8 in.) length of elastic between the body elastics for the front legs. Onto the body elastics thread two 12 cm (4¾ in.) and six 14 cm (5½ in.) circles then pass a 20 cm (8 in.) length of elastic between the body elastics for the back legs. To complete the body, thread on one 12 cm (4¾ in.), one 11 cm (4⅜ in.), one 10 cm (4 in.) and one 9 cm (3⅝ in.) circle. Knot the folded end of the body elastic, trimming off any excess length. Make the tail and sew it in place as given for the tiger.

Onto each front leg elastic, thread thirteen 8 cm (3¼ in.) circles. Onto each back leg elastic, thread two 10 cm (4 in.), two 9 cm (3⅝ in.) and eight 8 cm (3¼ in.) circles. Knot the ends of the elastics, trimming off any excess length. To hold these knots in place, cut an 8 cm (3¼ in.) diameter circle for each leg but do not snip a hole in the centre. Run a gathering thread round each circle and pull up the gathers, having a knotted end of elastic in the centre of each circle. Finish off the threads, oversewing securely through the centres of the circles and the elastic. Catch the edges of these circles to each other with a few stitches at the front and back legs where they touch so that the elephant will stand upright.

Pencil toppers

These fun characters for popping onto the ends of pencils can also be used as mini stick puppets. Table tennis balls are used for the heads.

Materials required
A table tennis ball for each character
Scraps of fabrics, felt trimmings, thin card (or cardboard), ribbon and braid

Permanent marker pens and pencils for marking and colouring the faces
Adhesive

To make the basic head
Cut a 4.5 cm by 6 cm (1¾ in. by 2½ in.) strip of thin card and roll it tightly around the pencil, having the 6 cm (2½ in.) measurement going around the pencil.

PIRATE'S HAT

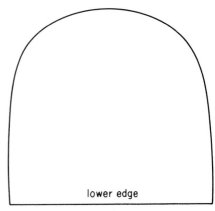

lower edge

GUARD'S HAT

Glue the strip as it is rolled taking care not to glue it to the pencil. Slip the cardboard tube off the pencil.

Now snip a hole in the table tennis ball just large enough to push the cardboard tube through. Spread one end of the tube with adhesive and push it right inside the ball, spreading the tube with adhesive at the other end where it passes through the hole in the ball. Mark on and colour the faces and hair using the illustration as a guide for each character.

To make the pirate

Glue a small felt patch over one eye, then tie a narrow strip of fabric or ribbon round the cardboard neck gluing it in place.

Cut two pirate hat pieces from felt. Cut the skull and crossbones shapes from white felt, and glue them to one of the hat pieces. Mark the eyes on the skull with marker pen. Glue one hat piece to the front of the head and one to the back, sticking the pieces together at each side.

To make the artist

For the cap cut a 10 cm (4 in.) diameter circle of fabric. Run a gathering thread round the edge and pull up the gathers leaving a 3 cm (1¼ in.) diameter hole at the centre. Spread the gathered raw edges with adhesive and stick the cap to one side of the head. Stick the remainder of the cap to the head where it touches.

Make a tassle from a few strands of thread and sew it to the centre of the cap. Glue a large ribbon bow to the neck at the front.

To make the guard

Stick a strip of red felt around the neck and also a bit of gold braid. Glue a strip of gold braid under the chin and up each side of the face for the chin strap.

Cut two hat pieces from black fur fabric or felt, and oversew or whip stitch the edges together, leaving the lower edges open. Turn the hat right side out and glue it to the head.

Four glove puppets

Jack and Jill, Santa Claus and the Christmas tree fairy are all constructed in the same basic way, and each completed puppet measures 28 cm (11 in.) from head to toe. The heads and legs are stuffed, and the lower edges of the bodies are attached to tubes of black fabric which fit over the arm when working the puppets.

The one-piece pink felt body is made by the stitch-around method, and 3 mm (1/8 in.) seams are allowed on all the other basic puppet pieces. Seams of 5 mm (1/4 in.) are allowed on all the clothing pieces unless otherwise stated.

Materials required for each basic puppet

Two 20 cm (8 in.) squares of pink felt. Note that a little more is required for the fairy to make the legs

For the black glove, a 24 cm by 30 cm (9½ in. by 12 in.) piece of black fabric

For the facial features, black and red felt, red thread and red pencil

Small amount of knitting wool for the hair

A little stuffing

Small pieces of fabrics, felt and trimmings for the legs and clothes

Scraps of white fur fabric for Santa Claus

Thin card (cardboard), clear adhesive (Scotch) tape and glue or adhesive such as UHU or Elmer's Glue.

To make the basic puppet

Trace the body pattern off the page onto thin paper, then cut it out. Pin the pattern onto two squares of pink felt. Trim the felt even with the lower edge of the pattern. Now stitch all round close to the edge of the pattern, leaving the lower edges open and a gap in the stitching at the top of the head as shown on the pattern. Trim the felt close to the pattern above the gap in the stitching. Remove the pattern and cut out the puppet close to the stitching line.

Turn the puppet right side out, then run a gathering thread round the neck at the position shown on the pattern, but do not pull up the gathers. Cut a 5 cm by 10 cm (2 in. by 4 in.) strip of card. Roll the card up along the length to form a 3 cm (1⅛ in.) diameter tube, 5 cm (2 in.) in length. Hold the end of the card in place with adhesive tape. Cover one end of the card tube by fixing strips of adhesive tape over it. Slip the tube inside the puppet's head positioning it as shown on the pattern. Pull up the gathering thread tightly to fit the tube then finish off.

Turn the body of the puppet inside out, taking it back over the head to expose the lower edge of the cardboard tube. Spread this end of the tube with adhesive, then turn the body right side out again and press the felt at the neck onto the glued portion of the tube to hold it in position.

Now stuff the head firmly through the top of the head, taking care to pack the stuffing all round the tube. Whip stitch the gap in the top of the head. Details of the faces and hair are given in the instructions for each individual puppet. The cheeks should be coloured by rubbing with the moistened tip of a red pencil.

To make a leg, first cut two foot pieces from felt or fabric. Join the pieces a little way along the centre front edges. Cut the leg from felt or fabric, placing the edge of the pattern indicated to a fold in the fabric. Join the lower edge of the leg to the top edge of the foot. Now join the centre back edges of the leg and the remainder of the foot seam. Trim the seam around the foot, turn the leg right side out and stuff firmly to within 2 cm (¾ in.) of the upper edge. Place a pin across the leg at this position to hold the stuffing in place as shown in diagram 1. Make the other leg in the same way. Note that when making Jack, the trouser pieces are sewn on the legs at this stage before sewing the legs in place on the body.

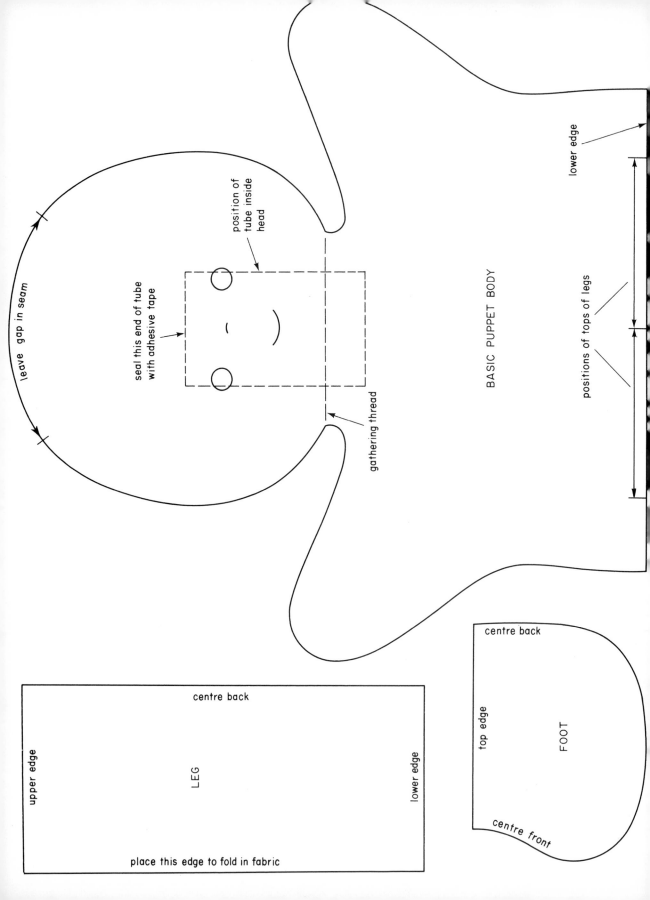

leave gap in seam

seal this end of tube
with adhesive tape

position of tube inside
head

gathering thread

BASIC PUPPET BODY

lower edge

positions of tops of legs

centre back

upper edge

LEG

lower edge

place this edge to fold in fabric

centre back

top edge

FOOT

centre front

Place the legs at the front lower edge of the puppet as shown in diagram 1 then sew the tops of the legs in place. Join the 24 cm (9½ in.) edges of the piece of black fabric to form a tube. Hem one end of the tube and run a gathering thread round the other end. Now keeping the puppet's legs in the same position as in diagram 1, slip the tube wrong side out over the puppet so that the raw edge of the tube is even with the lower edge of the puppet body. Pull up the gathers in the tube to fit the body, then sew these edges together all round taking a 5 mm (¼ in.) seam as shown in diagram 2. Pull the tube down turning it right side out then remove the pins from the legs.

To make Jill

For the dress cut two 16 cm by 22 cm (6¼ in. by 8¾ in.) pieces of fabric. Join the pieces at the 16 cm (6¼ in.) edges for 9 cm (3½ in.) only, leaving 7 cm (2¾ in.) open at the tops of the seams for the armholes. Turn in and stitch down the armhole edges to neaten. Make a narrow hem on the lower edge of the dress and sew on the trimming. Turn in the remaining raw edges for the neck and run round a gather-ing thread. Put the dress on the puppet, pulling the arms through the armholes. Pull up the gathering thread round the neck and finish off. Space out the gathers evenly, then sew to the neck all round. Sew a ribbon bow to the front neck edge of the dress.

Cut small circles of black felt for the eyes and also mark the positions of the nose and mouth with pencil. Stick the eyes in place and work the mouth and nose in small stitches using red thread.

For the hair, first sew a few loops of wool to the forehead for a fringe. Cut twenty-one 40 cm (16 in.) lengths of wool, and sew the centre of the lengths to the head above the fringe. Take the strands of wool to each side of the head and sew them there in bunches. Plait the wool strands and tie thread round the ends of the plaits to hold them in place.

Cut the cap from fabric, placing the edge indicated on the pattern to a fold in the fabric. Take a narrow hem all round the edge of the cap. Place the face edge of the cap on the puppet just lapping the hair. Sew the points marked A together at the back of the head. Catch the remaining point B to the A points then sew the face edge of the cap to the head all round.

To make Jack

Make the legs in the usual way, then for each pants leg cut an 8 cm by 12 cm (3 in. by 4¾ in.) strip of fabric. Join the 8 cm (3 in.) edges, then leaving the wrong side outside, run a gathering thread round one raw edge. Slip this gathered edge on the leg tak-ing it up over the foot, then pull up the gathers to fit the leg and fasten off. Turn the pants leg right side out, up over the leg, placing the top raw edge even with the top of the leg. Gather this upper edge to fit the leg then tack all the top edges together. Now sew the legs in position.

Make the face in the same way as for Jill. For the hair cut a 3 cm by 18 cm (1¼ in by 7 in.) strip of thick paper. Wind wool around the strip to cover it com-pletely. Stitch through the wool strands along one long edge, cut through the wool loops at the other long edge, then pull away the paper strip. Sew this fringe across the forehead and round the sides of the head as illustrated. The remainder of the head is covered by the cap.

For the shirt cut two 13 cm by 22 cm (5 in. by 8¾ in.) pieces of fabric. Join the 13 cm (5 in.) edges for 7 cm (2¾ in.) leaving 6 cm (2¼ in.) open at the top for the armholes. Turn in and stitch down the armhole edges to neaten. Now join the top edges for 2 cm (¾ in.) at each side, forming the shoulder seams. Hem the lower edge of the shirt then gather the neck edge and sew to the puppet as for Jill.

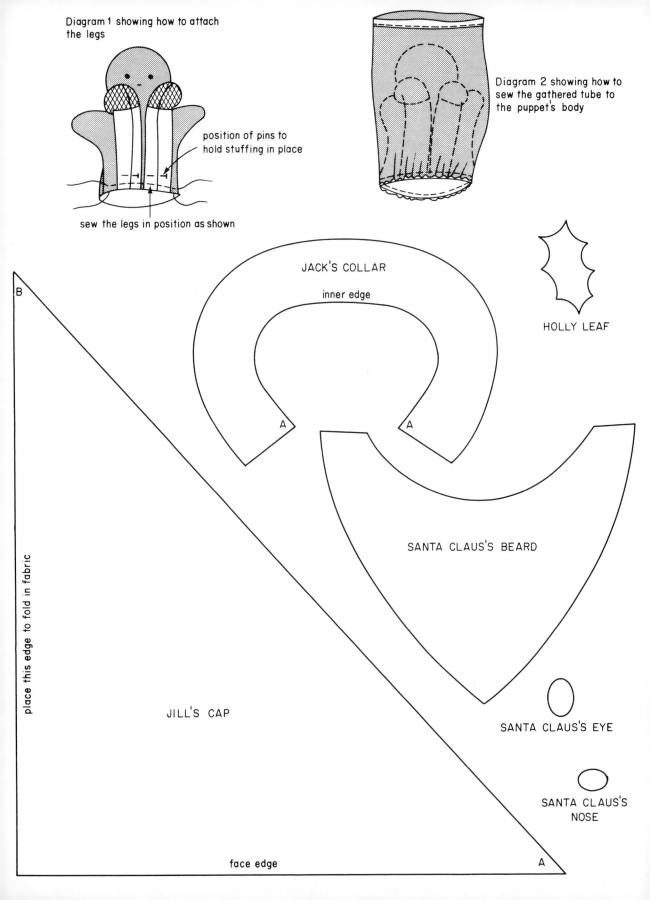

Diagram 1 showing how to attach the legs

position of pins to hold stuffing in place

sew the legs in position as shown

Diagram 2 showing how to sew the gathered tube to the puppet's body

JACK'S COLLAR

inner edge

HOLLY LEAF

B

A   A

SANTA CLAUS'S BEARD

place this edge to fold in fabric

JILL'S CAP

SANTA CLAUS'S EYE

SANTA CLAUS'S NOSE

face edge   A

Jack

Santa Claus

Cut the collar from felt. Spread a little adhesive round the inner edge of the collar and place it around the puppet's neck. Catch the points marked A together at the centre front then sew on a ribbon bow.

For the cap cut a 16 cm (6¼ in.) diameter circle of fabric. Turn in the edge and gather it to fit the head, lapping it over the top of the hair. Cut a 1 cm (⅜ in.) wide strip of felt long enough to go round the gathered edge of the hat. Sew one edge of this strip to the hat lapping it slightly over the gathers. Place the hat on the head and sew the lower edge of the band in place.

To make Santa Claus

Make the basic puppet using red fabric for the legs and grey fabric for the feet.

For the coat cut two 16 cm by 22 cm (6¼ in. by 8¾ in.) strips of red fabric. Make as for Jack's shirt leaving 6 cm (2¼ in.) open for the armholes and joining 3 cm (1¼ in.) at each end of the top edges for the shoulder seams. Cut 1 cm (⅜ in.) wide strips of

white fur fabric and stick these round the armholes and lower edges of the coat and also round the top edges of the feet. Run a gathering thread round the coat about 7 cm (2¾ in.) up from the lower edge and pull up the gathers to measure 28 cm (11 in.) all round. Sew a strip of braid round the gathers. Gather the neck edge of the coat, and sew it in place as for Jack's shirt.

Cut the eyes from black felt and the nose from red felt, then stick them in place. Cut the beard from white fur fabric then stick it to the face below the nose.

For the hood cut a 9 cm by 22 cm (3½ in. by 8¾ in.) strip of red fabric. Fold it, bringing the 9 cm (3½ in.) edges together, then join the raw edges of one 22 cm (8¾ in.) edge for the centre back of the hood. Gather the remaining 22 cm (8¾ in.) edge to fit around the puppet's face. Turn in and gather the remaining raw edge to fit round the back of the neck. Put the hood on the head and sew the gathered neck edge to the neck edge of the coat. Sew the gathered face edge round the face. Stick a 2 cm (¾ in.) wide strip of fur

Christmas tree fairy

To make the fairy

Make the legs from pink felt to match the body, and the feet from the same fabric as used for the dress. Make the face in the same way as for Jill.

For the hair cut about twenty 30 cm (12 in.) lengths of wool. Sew the centres of the wool strands to the forehead. Take the strands down to each side of the head level with the mouth and sew them there. Take the strands to the centre back of the head and sew them there, then sew the ends of the wool down, tucking them under the strands of wool. Repeat this whole process behind the first lot of wool strands. Finally, to cover the top of the head, sew on a small twisted hank of wool for a bun.

For the headdress, sew two rows of silver tinsel around the bun, then stick a strip of braid around the head, just below the tinsel.

Make the dress in the same way as given for Jill, but before gathering the neck edge, run a gathering thread across the dress 4 cm (1½ in.) down from the neck edge at the front and back. Pull up each gather to measure 10 cm (4 in.) and fasten off. Sew trimming round the lower edge of the dress.

For the wings cut two 12 cm by 22 cm (4¾ in. by 8¾ in.) pieces of transparent or net fabric. Join the pieces round the edges taking a 3 mm (⅛ in.) seam and leaving a gap in the seam for turning. Turn right side out and slip stitch the gap. Gather through the centre of the wings across the 12 cm (4¾ in.) width. Pull up the gathers tightly and fasten off, then sew this gathered centre to the centre back of the dress, just below the neck. Catch a wing to each arm with a few stitches.

fabric round the face edge of the hood. Cut two holly leaf shapes from green felt and a few small circles of red felt for berries. Stick these to the hood as shown.

Fortune-telling gypsy doll

Fortune-telling dolls similar to the one illustrated were very popular in the Victorian era, and Queen Victoria as a child owned one of these. It had a skirt composed of folded pieces of paper with the mottoes written in ink.

The doll illustrated stands 25 cm (10 in.) high and is very easy to make from household odds and ends. The doll's skirt is made from eighty-four folded coloured paper leaves, each one concealing a prediction for the future. The upper half of the doll is spun around with a twist of the fingers, and when it stops, the pointer indicates which leaf is to be unfolded. To open up the leaf, flatten it right out then pull the upturned point forward to reveal the fortune.

The whole family could participate in preparing the fortunes and these would be especially entertaining if written in verse. Alternatively, horoscopes can be cut from magazines and newspapers and glued to the leaves, omitting the various birth signs.

Materials required

Four ordinary sewing cotton reels (thread spools), either wooden or plastic

A sharpened pencil, measuring 14.5 cm (5¾ in.) in length. Note that the pencil can be cut to this length if necessary

A table tennis ball for the doll's head

Strong craft, or poster paper in various colours for the paper leaves

Scraps of fabrics, trimmings, cotton wad (cotton wool), cuttings off nylon stocking or tights, thin card (cardboard), knitting wool, gold gift wrapping braid, a cocktail stick

Black and red pens or pencils for marking on the doll's face

Adhesive

To make the skirt

For the centre spindle, glue three of the cotton reels together on top of each other. On the top cotton reel stick a circle of card cut to fit. Glue the remaining cotton reel on top of this card circle. Cut a strip of thin card to fit right round the cotton reels to cover them all completely. Glue the card securely round the reels.

Push the unsharpened end of the pencil inside the centre hole of the top cotton reel. If the pencil does not fit tightly, remove it, then glue a strip of paper or thin card round it to make it fit the hole.

For the paper leaves which form the doll's skirt, trace the pattern off the page, cut it out, then stick it onto a piece of thin card. Cut out the card even with the paper pattern. Now use this as a template to draw round onto the coloured paper which is to be used for the skirt.

Cut about eighty-four leaves, then write or stick the prediction at the position shown on the pattern. Bend up the lower portion of one leaf along the first fold line then fold the leaf in half on the second fold line at the centre. Fold another leaf in the same way. Keeping the two leaves in the folded position, stick them together as shown in the diagram, spreading adhesive all round the edges only.

Continue folding the leaves and gluing them all together in this way until there are enough to go round the cotton reel spindle. To fix the skirt to the spindle, spread adhesive liberally round the top 4 cm (1½ in.) of the spindle, then place the skirt around it pressing the centre back edges of the leaves carefully onto the glued portion until they are securely stuck in place.

To make the doll

For the head, take the table tennis ball and cut out a hole large enough to slip easily over the pencil point. Cut the body from thin card. Bend it into a

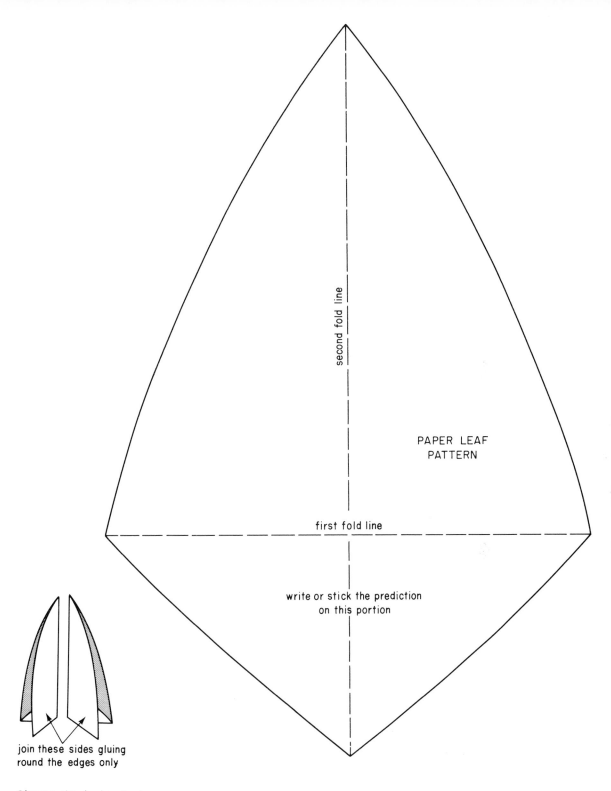

second fold line

PAPER LEAF
PATTERN

first fold line

write or stick the prediction
on this portion

join these sides gluing
round the edges only

Diagram showing how to glue
the first two leaves together

Try to be tactful with those who are close to you. Friends could be rather unco-operative and this may result in having to postpone a decision. A disturbing week, so tread carefully.

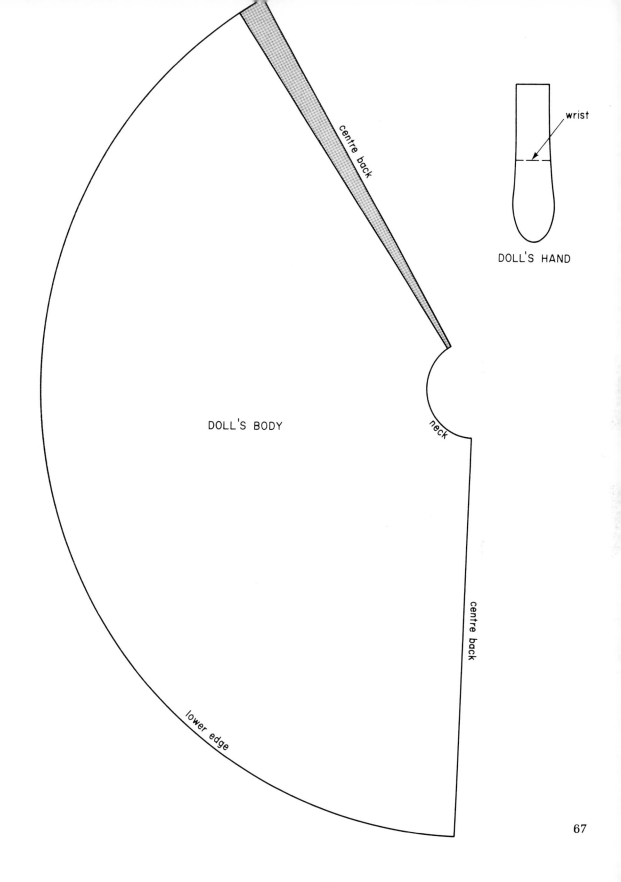

centre back

DOLL'S HAND

wrist

DOLL'S BODY

neck

centre back

lower edge

67

The upper and lower halves separated

cone-shape, lapping and sticking one centre back edge over the shaded portion of the other back edge. Glue the neck edge of the body just inside the hole in the head making the hole a little larger if necessary. Cover the head by pulling a double thickness of nylon stocking fabric over it, then gather and tie the fabric in position round the neck with thread. Trim off the excess fabric and glue the raw edges onto the cardboard body.

Cover the cardboard body by gluing on a piece of fabric cut to the same shape as the body pattern. Glue trimming round the neck and lower edges of the body. Cut two hands from card using the pattern. Wrap a little cotton wool round each hand, then cover them with nylon stocking fabric as for the head, tying it in place round the wrists. For each sleeve cut an 8 cm by 11 cm (3 in. by 4¼ in.) strip of fabric. Overlap the 11 cm (4¼ in.) edges of each one a little bit and stick. Turn in the raw edge at one end of each sleeve a little and run round gathering threads. Slip a hand inside each gathered edge and pull up and stick the gathers to the wrists. Pad each sleeve by pushing in a little cotton wool, then gather and stick the remaining raw edges to each side of the doll about 1 cm (⅜ in.) down from the neck.

For the shawl cut an 18 cm (7 in.) square of fabric. Fray out the raw edges a little, then fold the shawl into a triangle and drape it around the doll as illustrated. Stick the shawl in place. Now bend the arms, and glue them to the body where they touch, to hold them in position as shown in the illustration. Glue the cocktail stick to the doll's right hand as shown, bending the hand around the stick. When the doll is placed in position over the pencil, the cocktail stick should be close to, but not touching, the paper leaves on the skirt.

Use pens or pencils to mark on the face as illustrated. For the hair, tie a few lengths of wool together at the centres then glue the centre to the forehead. Glue the wool strands down each side of the face and towards the back of the head. Stick small loops of gold gift wrapping braid to each side of the head just beneath the hair, for the earrings.

For the headscarf cut a 12 cm (4¾ in.) square of fabric. Fold it into a triangle then glue it in position on the doll's head as shown in the illustration.

Bread dough miniatures

A wide range of miniature objects can be modelled from bread dough consisting of a mixture of plain flour, salt and water. Children will particularly like the doll-sized food and complete meals on a plate, and these can also be made into amusing brooches and pendants.

The items are baked in a very slow oven to get a hard and fairly durable finish. After this they can be sealed with clear varnish or painted with coloured enamel paints of the type used on plastic model soliders, ships and aeroplanes.

Materials required
Plain flour, salt and water for the dough
Clear polyurethane varnish, either glossy or matt, and coloured enamel paints

Cups and saucers, plates of food and fruit

Small metal lids off coffee or cocoa tins
Brooch back fittings and epoxy adhesive
Strong cord and a jump ring for the pendant

To make the dough

The ingredients should be mixed in the following proportions: three measures of flour to one of salt to one of water. Begin by making a small quantity of dough at a time using, say, a tablespoon as the measure. Work the dough together, and if it feels too dry add a little more water. If too wet, work in a little more flour. Now knead the dough for about fifteen minutes until it is very smooth. The dough should be pliable, but firm enough to hold the shape when pinched.

When making each item, work each piece of dough smooth before using it. To stick pieces of dough together, dab a little water on the surfaces to be joined. When modelling in a warm atmosphere, put the unused dough in a plastic bag to prevent it from drying out.

To bake the miniatures

Place the items on a flat baking pan covered with lightly oiled foil paper. The largest items, such as the roast turkey which is 6 cm (2¼ in.) long, will tend to crack if baked too quickly. Bake such items at first in a very slow oven at 90°C (200°F) (or Gas mark ¼) for about three hours to dry out gradually. Increase the temperature to 120°C (250°F) (or Gas mark ½) for the next hour and finally bake for an hour at 150°C (300°F)(or Gas mark 2). Lift up the items from time to time to see if they are hardening underneath. For the small items illustrated, bake at about 150°C (300°F)(Gas mark 2) for one hour and a further hour at 180°C (350°F)(Gas mark 4).

For a well baked effect on loaves, pies, etc., place the baked items under a hot broiler or grill for a minute or two.

When baked items are cool they can be smoothed by rubbing with sandpaper if necessary. If any of the miniatures with flat bases have risen slightly, the bases can be sandpapered to flatten them. Flatten the backs of brooches in this way before gluing on the brooch fittings.

The plates of food, cups and saucers, and fruit should be painted with enamel paints in the appro-

The tiny teddies

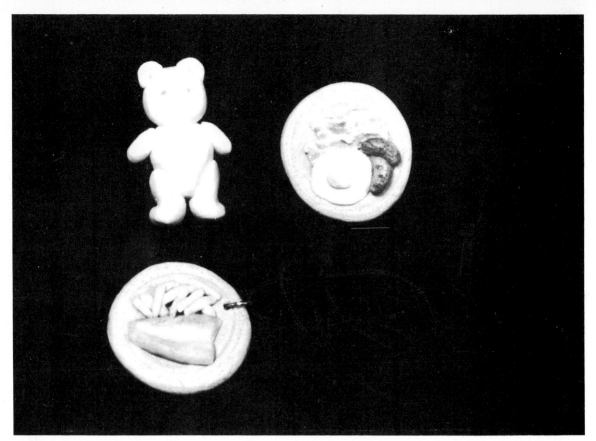

Teddy brooch, novelty brooch and pendant

priate colours. All baked items are finally painted with two or three coats of varnish.

To make the tiny teddies
Roll a ball of dough about 2 cm (¾ in.) in diameter for the body. Place it on the baking tray pressing it down to flatten the base. Coax the dough into a domed shape. Make a slightly smaller ball of dough and stick it on top of the body.

Take a pinch of dough for each ear, and roll into a small oval shape. Fix these to the head. Pinch, to flatten the ears slightly, then push a pencil point in the centre of each to make small depressions. Make the facial features with the pencil point also. Roll small ovals of dough for the legs, and slightly smaller ones for the arms, then stick them to the body as illustrated.

To make the teddy brooch
Roll a 2.5 cm (1 in.) diameter ball of dough. Place it on a baking tray and flatten slightly. Make the leg 'sockets' by pinching the dough between finger and thumb. Fix on a smaller flattened ball of dough for the head and ovals for the ears. To make the snout, smooth a small lump of dough into the centre of the face then shape it to a point for the nose. Mark the eyes, nose and ears with a pencil point. Fix on small ovals for the arms and larger ovals for the legs. Turn up the ends of the legs for the feet. After baking and varnishing, glue the brooch fitting to the back.

To make the plates of food
Flatten a 2.5 cm (1 in.) diameter ball of dough, then use the base of a cup or small bottle to impress the centre of the plate, forming a rim round the edge. Model the fish and chips, bacon, egg and sausages as shown in the illustrations then fix them to the plates.

Make a small hole in the plate before baking, if it is to be used for a pendant.

To make the cups and saucers
For the cups use 2 cm (¾ in.) diameter balls of dough. Model each cup carefully over a fingertip then fix on a tiny strip of dough for a handle. Make

Top **Humpty Dumpty game**

Bottom **Hansel, Gretel and the wicked witch**

Turkey, pies, bread and cakes

the saucers in the same way as for the plates but smaller.

To make the fruit

Make the grapefruit about 1.5 cm (½ in.) in diameter and the oranges, apples and pears a little smaller, tapering the pears at one end. Impress the stalk ends of the fruit with the point of a pencil. Roll long ovals of dough for the bananas and bend to curve them, then fix several together.

To make the pie, bread and cakes

For the flat pie, fill a small metal lid with dough, pressing it onto the edges of the lid. Trim off the dough round the edge with a knife. Snip the centre holes with scissors and make impressions round the edge with the side of a pencil point. Bake the pie in the lid.

For the swiss roll, roll out a strip of dough, cut out a neat oblong shape, then roll it up.

Make the loaves and pork pie as illustrated.

For the cherry cake make a flat disc-shape about 4 cm (1½ in.) in diameter and 1.5 cm (½ in.) deep.

To make the turkey

Roll a 3.5 cm (1½ in.) diameter ball of dough into an oval shape and flatten it slightly onto the baking tray. Pinch the top to form the breast bone. Roll small ovals for the wings, larger ovals for the legs and fix them in place, tapering the legs at one end as shown in the illustration.

The hamsters, a family of mascots

These mini-hamsters are just 8 cm (3 in.) high, and baby hamster has a pram (or baby carriage) made from a very small cardboard box (such as a small matchbox tray). While they are not of course suitable for very young children to play with, older children and adults should enjoy owning these little furry creatures as mascots or ornaments.

The basic pattern is a simple cone-shape, and when first stuffed this does not look at all like the finished animal. The entire hamster-like effect is achieved by a thread tied round the body to make the neck, by a gathering thread used to bring the head forward, and also by sewing the beads for the eyes tightly into the head.

Seams and turnings of 3 mm (⅛ in.) are allowed on all the clothes pieces.

Materials required for the hamsters

Small pieces of fawn fleecy fabric and fawn felt to match the fleece as closely as possible

For the adults' eyes, 6 mm (¼ in.) diameter shiny black beads, and slightly smaller beads for the baby

For the whiskers, invisible nylon sewing thread

Small amount of stuffing

Small lumps of Plasticine for weighting the bases of the hamsters

For the clothes, scraps of fabrics, ribbons, lace edging and trimmings

For the spectacles, medium gauge fuse wire (or very thin wire)

For the baby carriage, a tiny box (matchbox tray), braid or trimming about 2 cm (¾ in.) wide, pipe cleaner, scraps of fabric, four 2 cm (¾ in.) diameter buttons

For grandmother's knitting, two plastic cocktail sticks and thick embroidery thread

For father's newspaper, cuttings of very small print from a magazine

For grandfather's walking stick, a pipe cleaner and piece of shoe lace

For grandfather's cap, a lid off a tube of chocolate beans or a thick button about 2 cm (¾ in.) in diameter

For grandfather's watch, a gold sequin and length of gold thread

Adhesive

To make the basic hamster

Cut the body piece from fleecy fabric. Oversew the front edges together and across the nose, pulling the stitches up tight so that the finished seam measures 8 cm (3 in.). Turn the body right side out and stuff firmly. Run a gathering thread round the lower edge. Take a ball of Plasticine about 1 cm (⅜ in.) in diameter, flatten it, then wrap a bit of stuffing round it. Place the Plasticine inside the gathered lower edge of the body, then pull up the gathers tightly and finish off. Pick out the fleece trapped in the front seam with the point of a pin so that the seam is hardly visible.

Stick a pin in the body at the front seam 4 cm (1½ in.) down from the nose. Tie a double strand of sewing thread tightly round the body at this position to make the neck, then remove the pin. To bring the head forward, use a double strand of sewing thread and take tiny running stitches from the neck to the nose through the front seam. Pull the thread up very tightly and finish off. Now sew the beads in place at each side of the head, 1.5 cm (½ in.) back from the nose, taking the thread through the head

from one bead to the other and pulling it up tightly to depress the beads into the head. Fasten off the thread. The hamster should now have the characteristic 'pouch' effect below the eyes at each side of the head.

Cut two ears from felt. Fold each ear in half at the dotted line shown on the pattern, and glue the lower edge as folded. Glue the lower edges of the ears in place on the head just behind each eye, pushing pins into the ears and head to hold them in place until the adhesive dries.

The feet and hands are made from double felt. Glue two layers of felt securely together and allow the adhesive to dry before cutting out. Cut two feet from the felt. Using small sharp scissors, snip the toe ends of the feet into four points as shown by the dotted lines on the pattern. If necessary, spread a little adhesive on the points, leave until tacky, then mould and press the felt to form neat points. Spread the back portion of the feet with adhesive then position them under the hamster as illustrated, having only the toe ends visible at the front. Catch the feet in place under the hamster with a few stitches.

Cut the tail from fleece and oversew the side edges together, having the right side of the fleece outside. Pin the lower edge of the tail in position at the back of the hamster, tucking it a little way under the base, then sew it in place.

Cut two arm pieces from fleece. Oversew the side edges of each arm together having the right side outside and pulling the stitches tight to curve the arm slightly. Make the hands in the same way as for the feet. Now glue the top edge of each hand inside the lower edge of each arm. Sew the arms in place as given in the instructions which follow for each hamster.

For the whiskers use four strands of nylon sewing thread. Knot the strands about 6 cm (2¼ in.) from one end, then use a needle to take the other ends of the strands through the nose. Knot the threads at the other side. Cut the whiskers to even lengths at each side.

To make father

For the sweater cut a 3 cm (1⅛ in.) wide strip of stretchy fabric, long enough to go round the body. Turn in one long raw edge and glue down to neaten. Join the short edges of the strip. Put the sweater on the hamster and tie a thread round the neck 1 cm (⅜ in.) below the top raw edge of the sweater. Roll down the 1 cm (⅜ in.) for the collar. Now sew the tops of the arms to each side of the body near to the

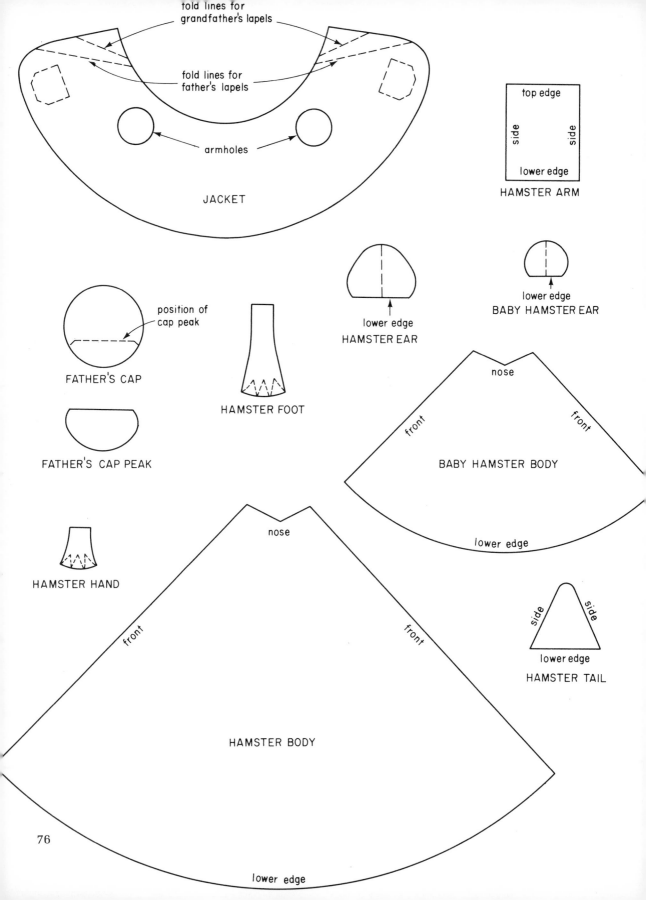

fold lines for
grandfather's lapels

fold lines for
father's lapels

armholes

JACKET

top edge

side   side

lower edge

HAMSTER ARM

lower edge
HAMSTER EAR

lower edge
BABY HAMSTER EAR

position of
cap peak

FATHER'S CAP

HAMSTER FOOT

nose

front   front

BABY HAMSTER BODY

lower edge

FATHER'S CAP PEAK

HAMSTER HAND

nose

front   front

side   side

lower edge

HAMSTER TAIL

HAMSTER BODY

76

lower edge

neck, taking the stitches through the sweater and into the body.

Cut the cap and cap peak pieces from thin card. Stick them onto a piece of felt, then cut out the felt a little larger all round than the card. Turn the extra felt to the other side of the card and stick down. Now stick the peak in place under the cap as shown by the dotted line on the cap pattern.

Cut the jacket from felt and use sharp pointed scissors to cut out the armhole circles. Cut two pockets from felt and glue in place as shown by the dotted lines on the jacket pattern. Fold back the lapels as shown on the pattern and glue them down, then place the jacket on the hamster and stick the fronts to the sweater.

Fold up the magazine cutting to measure about 1 cm by 3.5 cm (⅜ in. by 1⅜ in.) then stick it under father's arm.

To make mother
For the hat, glue on a large guipure flower or a bit of gathered lace, and glue on rosebuds or other flower trimming.

For the dress cut a 3.5 cm by 16 cm (1⅜ in. by 6¼

Father hamster

Mother and baby hamster

Grandfather hamster

in.) strip of fabric. Glue lace trim to one long edge, then lap and stick the short edges. Turn in the remaining raw edge and run round a gathering thread. Put the dress on the hamster, pull up the gathers round the neck and fasten off. Sew the arms in place as for father. Glue lace trim round the neck and a ribbon bow to the front neck edge.

To make grandfather

Sew the tops of the arms to each side of the body just below the neck. For the cravat cut a 16 cm (6¼ in.) length of ribbon and tie it round the neck, then stick the ends to the body at the front.

Make the jacket as for father gluing down the smaller lapels as shown on the pattern. Enclose the sequin and one end of the gold thread when gluing on the left pocket. Put the jacket on the hamster, then use a needle to take the gold thread through the right front edge of the jacket and glue it in place as illustrated.

For the cap, glue a piece of felt onto the lid or button, stretching it to cover completely. Trim the felt even with the lid or button all round, then stick a bit of braid round as illustrated.

For the spectacles, bend the wire round a pencil to make each lens, leaving a 1 cm (⅜ in.) length between the two. Trim off the ends of the wire, then bend the 1 cm (⅜ in.) to an inverted U-shape and stick this portion to the hamster's nose.

For the walking stick cut a 5 cm (2 in.) length of pipe cleaner. Push this inside a bit of shoe lace. Seal the ends of the shoe lace with glue, pressing all the raw edges together. Bend the top of the walking stick to the correct shape, and stick this to the hamster's hand.

To make grandmother

Make the dress as for mother's, omitting the bow and lace trim at the neck. Sew the arms in place as for mother.

For the shawl cut an 8 cm (3¼ in.) square of fabric. Fray out all the raw edges a little. Fold the shawl into a triangle and place it round the hamster's shoulders, gluing the ends in place at the front as illustrated.

Make the spectacles as for grandfather's, bending the wire round a smaller shape than the pencil, for example a knitting needle.

78

Grandmother hamster

Cut the plastic cocktail sticks to 5 cm (2 in.) in length. Carefully warm the cut ends near a match flame until the plastic softens, then flatten to make the knob ends of the knitting needles. Cast a few stitches on the needles using the embroidery thread, then work a few rows. Wind the end of the thread into a ball using adhesive to hold the thread in place. Glue the knitting to the hamster's hands and arms as illustrated.

To make the baby and pram

Make the baby body as for the adult body, omitting the Plasticine, and tying the thread round 2 cm (¾ in.) below the nose. Make the ears and glue in place as for the adults. Sew the eyes in position 1 cm (⅜ in.) back from the nose. Glue a bit of fabric round the baby for a shawl. Note that it is not necessary to make the arms, feet and tail on the baby. Glue a bit of gathered lace round the head for a bonnet and a ribbon bow under the chin.

Glue trimming round the sides of the little box then glue two buttons to each side as illustrated. For the pram handle cut an 8 cm (3¼ in.) length of pipe cleaner. Roll this up inside a length of trimming to match the pram, gluing the trimming in place. Bend the handle to shape, and glue the ends inside the pram at each front corner as illustrated. Fold a small piece of fabric for a pillow and glue it in place. Glue the baby into the pram, then glue a piece of fabric on top for a coverlet.

'Cries of London' peg dolls

Pedlars of all kinds of goods were once a familiar sight in the streets of London. The four dolls shown here were inspired by eighteenth century prints of paintings by Francis Wheatley. Wheatley did a series of London cries in the 1790s. The pedlars are selling oranges, love songs, strawberries and matches. Each doll, just 12 cm (4¾ in.) high is made from an old-fashioned wooden clothes peg (or dolly peg).

The fabrics used for the costumes should be thin soft cotton which will crease easily. Cuttings from old hankerchiefs are ideal for this purpose. To make the garments drape properly on the dolls, first fix them in place, then wet the fabric, smooth it into natural folds and creases, and leave to dry. All the dolls are made in the same basic way with slight variations in draping and garment sizes.

Plain brown furnishing (finishing) braid is used for the pedlars' baskets since the wrong side usually has a most suitable basket-like texture.

ture. The fruit can be made from Plasticine or self-hardening modelling clay.

Overlaps and turnings of 5 mm (¼ in.) are allowed unless otherwise stated.

Materials required for each doll

One clothes peg and one pipe cleaner

Scraps of fabrics, ribbon, nylon stocking or tights fabric, knitting wool for hair, cotton wool, brown furnishing (finishing) braid, thin card and paper

Plasticine, or self-hardening modelling clay and enamel paints

Fine sandpaper

Coloured pencils for marking on the faces

Adhesive

To make the match girl

The cry for this pedlar was 'Do you want any Matches?'.

Rub the top of the peg with sandpaper to make it quite smooth. Take a small piece of cotton wad and tie it with sewing thread to the front of the doll 1 cm (⅜ in.) below the neck, then overlap and stick the wad right around the doll at the position of the hips as shown in diagram 1.

For the bodice cut a 3 cm by 7 cm (1¼ in. by 2¾ in.) strip of fabric. Wrap the strip around the doll 1 cm (⅜ in.) below the neck, then overlap the stick the short edges trimming off any excess fabric. Run a gathering thread round the upper edge of the bodice then pull up the gathers to fit the peg and finish off. Tie a thread tightly around the bodice at the waist between the two cotton wad pads.

For the underskirt cut an 8 cm by 18 cm (3⅛ in. by 7 in.) strip of fabric. Turn in one long edge and glue down to neaten for the hem. Overlap the short edges of the strip and stick, then turn in the remaining raw edge and run round a gathering thread.

Now take a small lump of Plasticine or modelling clay and push the ends of the peg right into it, thus forming a base so that the doll will stand upright without support. Put the underskirt on the doll, pull up the gathers round the waist, and finish off, taking care that the hem edge of the skirt touches the ground.

For the overskirt cut a piece of fabric as for the underskirt. Turn in one long edge and both short edges and glue down to neaten. Turn in and gather the remaining raw edge round the doll's waist having the short edges at the centre front. Turn in

The match girl

the lower front corners of the overskirt and take them up inside the overskirt to the centre back waist of the doll, then glue them in this position.

For the apron cut an 8 cm by 9 cm (3⅛ in. by 3½ in.) strip of fabric. Turn in all the edges and stick down except for one 9 cm (3½ in.) edge. Turn in and gather this edge, and stick it to the waist at the front. Lift one corner of the apron and stick it to one side of the waist. Glue a narrow strip of ribbon round the waist for the apron waistband.

For the arms cut the pipe cleaner to 15 cm (6 in.) in length, and bend round 1 cm (⅜ in.) at each end for the hands. Tie a little cotton wad round the arms to pad them out as shown in diagram 2. Trace the arm pattern off the page onto thin paper, then cut it out. Pin the pattern onto a double thickness of nylon stocking fabric, placing the edge indicated on the pattern to a fold in the fabric. Trim the fabric even with the top edge of the pattern. Now stitch round close to the edge of the pattern leaving the top edges open.

Remove the pattern and cut out the arm close to the stitching line. Turn the arm right side out and

slip it over one end of the pipe cleaner, then tie the top edges to the pipe cleaner with thread. Tie a thread round the arm at the position of the wrist. Cover the other end of the pipe cleaner in the same way.

For the sleeves cut a 3 cm by 9 cm (1⅛ in. by 3½ in.) strip of fabric. Turn in the short edges and stick down to neaten. Overlap and stick the long edges, then slip the sleeve onto the pipe cleaner arms having each end of the sleeve piece an equal distance from each hand. Tie a thread tightly round at the centre of the sleeve piece. Now glue this tied centre to the centre back of the doll just below the neck and bend the arms into position as illustrated.

For the neck scarf cut a 5 cm (2 in.) square of fabric. Turn in and stick all the raw edges. Fold the scarf into a triangle and glue it round the doll as illustrated.

Mark on the face as shown in diagram 3, slightly off centre so that the doll's head appears to be turned to one side. For the hair, cut short lengths of wool and pull them carefully apart to make very fine strands. Stick some strands across the forehead and down each side of the face, then stick some to the back of the head to hang down the back of the doll.

For the frilled cap cut a 10 cm (4 in.) length of tape or ribbon about 1.5 cm (½ in.) in width. Overlap and stick the short edges, then gather one long edge up tightly and fasten off. To pleat the cap, run a gathering thread round the remaining long edge, pull up the gathers very tightly and press the fabric with the fingers to crease it. Pull out the second gathering thread then stick the cap to the doll's head.

For the straw hat use fabric with a straw-like texture. Glue two layers of fabric together before cutting out the hat to prevent fraying. Cut out the hat using the pattern. Bring the edges together as indicated on the pattern and oversew them neatly. Turn the hat right side out and gently stretch the centre with the fingers, easing it into a rounded shape. Glue the hat to the doll's head on top of the frilled cap. Stick a strip of narrow ribbon over the top of the hat under the doll's chin as illustrated.

For the base of the basket cut a 2 cm (¾ in.) diameter circle of card. Glue a strip of braid about 1.5 cm (½ in.) in width round the base, lapping and sticking the short edges of the braid. For the basket handle pull a few threads from a bit of braid, spread them with adhesive then twist them all together. Stick the handle to the basket as illustrated.

To make the bundles of matches, cut a strip of card about postcard thickness, then snip all along one edge with scissors as shown in diagram 4. Cut

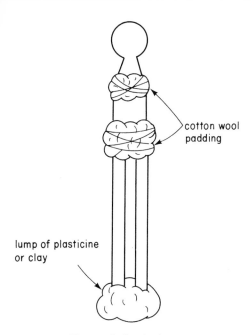

cotton wool padding

lump of plasticine or clay

Diagram 1 showing how to pad the body

Diagram 2 showing how to pad the pipe cleaner arms

Diagram 3 showing how to mark on the doll's face

Diagram 4 showing how to cut the matches from card

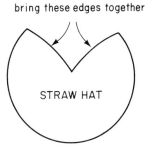

bring these edges together

STRAW HAT

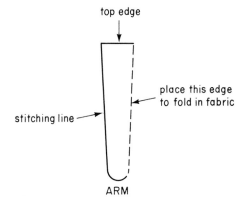

top edge

place this edge to fold in fabric

stitching line

ARM

off a few matches at a time making them about 1.5 cm (½ in.) in length then tie round a thread to make a bundle. Glue one bundle to the doll's hand and several bundles inside the basket.

To make the strawberry seller
The cry for this pedlar was 'Strawberrys Scarlet Strawberrys!'.

Make this doll as for the match girl with the following variations. Use an 8 cm by 24 cm (3⅛ in. by 9½ in.) strip for the underskirt and omit the over-skirt. Make the apron 8 cm by 12 cm (3⅛ in. by 4¾ in.).

Cross the front points of the neck scarf right over each other and glue them in place to form the 'tucked into the bodice' effect as illustrated. Glue ribbon round the crown of the straw hat as illustrated.

Make the base of the large basket 2.5 cm (1 in.) in diameter and use 2 cm (¾ in.) wide brown braid. Pack the base of the basket with paper and model only a few strawberries to glue on top. Mark the

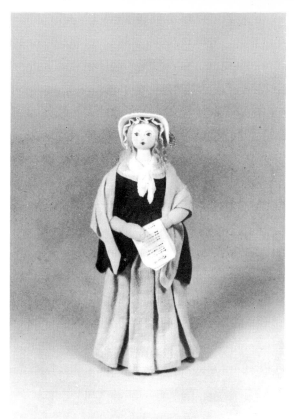

The strawberry seller

The pedlar of love songs

seeds on the strawberries with the point of a pin. Half cover the top of the basket by gluing on a small square of fabric as illustrated. Make two small handles and glue one to each side as shown.

Make a small tapered basket for the doll to carry, about 2 cm (¾ in.) in length, making the lower end 5 mm (¼ in.) in diameter.

To make the pedlar of love songs
The cry for this pedlar was 'A New Love Song only ha'penny a piece'.

Make as for the match girl with the following variations. Use an 8 cm by 24 cm (3⅛ in. by 9½ in.) piece of fabric for the underskirt. Bunch up the overskirt all round, sticking it in place. Omit the apron. Use a 10 cm (4 in.) square of fabric for the shawl, turn in and stick the raw edges, then fold into a triangle and drape around the doll as illustrated. Glue ribbon round the crown of the straw hat as illustrated.

For the song sheets cut a few 1.5 cm by 2.5 cm (⅝ in. by 1 in.) pieces of paper. Mark the top sheet as shown in the illustration then glue them all to the doll's hands as shown.

To make the orange vendor
The cry for this pedlar was 'Sweet China Oranges, sweet China'.

Make as for the match girl with the following variations. Make the neck scarf as for the strawberry seller. Use an 8 cm by 24 cm (3⅛ in. by 9½ in.) strip of fabric for the underskirt. Cut an 8 cm by 12 cm (3⅛ in. by 4¾ in.) piece for the apron and tuck both lower corners into the apron waistband at each side. Glue ribbon round the straw hat as illustrated.

Make the orange basket as for the large strawberry basket and stick a square of tissue paper inside before gluing in the oranges. Make the oranges about the size of peas and make indents in the tops with a pencil point.

The orange vendor

Mrs Caterpillar

Mrs Caterpillar, 26 cm (10 in.) in length, is very easy to make from gathered circles of fabric filled with stuffing and threaded onto elastic. The daisy parasol is made from felt with a pipe cleaner for the stalk. Seams and turnings of 5 mm (¼ in.) are allowed on all pieces unless otherwise stated.

Materials required
Small pieces of two different patterned fabrics for the body

Scraps of white fabric for the head and arms and patterned fabric for the scarf

Thin round elastic, 32 cm (12½ in.) in length

Brown permanent marker pen, red ball point pen, red pencil and black felt for the facial features

Small amount of stuffing

Scraps of green, white and yellow felt and one pipe cleaner for the daisy

Adhesive

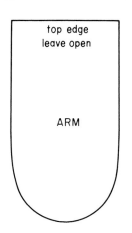

top edge
leave open

ARM

LEAF

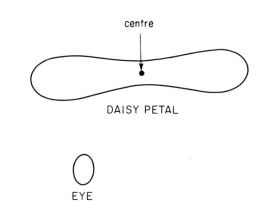

centre

DAISY PETAL

EYE

To make the caterpillar

Cut six 9 cm (3½ in.) diameter circles of each of the two patterned fabrics. Run a gathering thread all round the edge of one circle, pull up the gathers, and at the same time stuff the circle lightly. Before fastening off the thread, knot the end of the elastic, push the knot inside the gathered circle then finish off, catching the elastic securely in the stitching.

Snip a small hole in the centre of each of the remaining fabric circles then gather and stuff them as for the first circle. Thread the circles onto the elastic using a darning needle to take the elastic through the centre holes and the gathered edges. Knot the end of the elastic.

Cut four arm pieces from white fabric. Join the pieces in pairs around the edges leaving the top edges open. For each sleeve cut a 4 cm by 8 cm (1½ in. by 3¼ in.) strip of fabric. Join the short edges of each strip and turn right side out. Place a sleeve on each arm and gather one raw edge round the top of the arm, then oversew the sleeve fabric to the arm. Turn in the remaining raw edges of the sleeves and gather them, pulling up the gathers to fit the arms, then finish off.

Sew the tops of the arms to the top gathered body circle, positioning them at the angle shown in the illustration.

For the head cut a 12 cm (4¾ in.) diameter circle of white fabric. Gather as for the first body circle and stuff firmly, then slip the knot in the body elastic inside the head before fastening off the thread, catching the elastic in the stitching at the same time. Mark the hair on the head above the face area

as illustrated, using brown pen. Cut the eyes from black felt and stick them to the face. Mark the nose and mouth with red pen and colour the cheeks with red pencil.

For the headscarf cut a 14 cm (5½ in.) square of fabric. Fray out all the raw edges a little, then fold it into a triangle and arrange the scarf round the head sewing the corners below the face as illustrated. Catch the scarf to the head with a stitch or two here and there.

To make the daisy parasol

For the daisy stalk cut a 14 cm (5½ in.) length of pipe cleaner. Cut a 1 cm by 14 cm (⅜ in. by 5½ in.) strip of green felt. Fold the strip around the pipe cleaner and oversew or whip stitch the long edges of the felt together, then oversew across each end.

Cut six daisy petal pieces from white felt. Colour the tips of the petals with red pen or pencil if desired. Lay the centres of the petals on top of each other, fanning them out to form a complete circular shape. Sew the petals together through all the centres.

For the centre of the daisy cut a 4 cm (1½ in.) diameter circle of yellow felt. Run a gathering thread round the edge, put a little stuffing in the centre, then pull up the gathers tightly and fasten off. Sew the daisy centre to the petals. Bend round one end of the stalk to form a small circle and sew this underneath the petals. Cut the leaf shape from green felt and sew it to the stalk. Bend round the other end of the stalk to fit round the caterpillar's arm.

Miniature rag doll

This doll is 28 cm (11 in.) in height. Her blouse and cap are sewn in place but the pants, skirt and apron are all removeable so that they can be interchanged or all worn together. The doll is made by the stitch-around method. Seams and turnings of 5 mm (¼ in.) are allowed on all other pieces unless otherwise stated.

Materials required
Small pieces of pink and black cotton fabric for the doll

Small amount of stuffing

Scraps of black felt for the eyes and 4 ply knitting wool for the hair

Black and red pencil and red thread for the facial features

For the blouse, pants, cap and skirt, 25 cm (10 in.) of 91 cm (36 in.) wide plain fabric

For the apron, 16 cm (6½ in.) of 91 cm (36 in.) wide patterned fabric

Two snap fasteners

Lace edging, 1.5 m (1¾ yd) in length

Short length of narrow elastic or shirring elastic

Adhesive

To make the doll
Trace the body, arm and leg patterns off the page onto thin paper. Pin the body pattern onto a double thickness of pink fabric and trim the fabric even with the lower edge of the pattern. Stitch all round close to the edge of the pattern leaving the lower edges open. Remove the pattern and cut out the body 5 mm (¼ in.) away from the stitching line. Clip the seam at the neck at each side. Pull the two layers of fabric apart at the neck and stitch a small dart across the neck at the front and back as shown on the pattern. Turn the body right side out and stuff firmly, then turn in the lower edges 5 mm (¼ in.) and oversew or whip stitch them together.

Pin the arm pattern onto two layers of pink fabric then trim the fabric even with the upper edge of the pattern. Stitch round the pattern, cut it out and turn it as for the body. Make the legs as for the arms using black fabric. Stuff the arms and legs to within 3 cm (1¼ in.) of the upper edges. Turn in the upper edges of each arm, bringing the seams together, then oversew, pulling the stitches tightly to gather. Do not sew the arms to the body at this stage. Turn in the upper edges of the legs bringing the seams together, then oversew. Sew the tops of the legs to the lower edge of the body.

Cut the eyes from felt and stick them in position as shown on the pattern, then mark on the eyelashes with black pencil. Mark on the mouth and nose with red pencil, then work the mouth in small stitches using red thread. Colour the cheeks by rubbing gently with red pencil.

For the hair, first sew a few loops of wool to the forehead for a fringe. Cut about thirty 30 cm (12 in.) long strands of wool and back stitch the centre of the strands to the position shown on the body pattern. Take the wool strands down the sides of the head and towards the back of the head just above the neck. Sew the strands to the head in a bunch then trim the ends to an even length. The remainder of the head will be covered by the cap.

To make the blouse
For the body of the blouse cut a 9 cm by 18 cm (3½ in. by 7 in.) strip of plain fabric. Turn in one long edge and sew on lace edging. Join the short edges of the strip. Make a narrow hem on the remaining raw edge. Run a gathering thread round the lace trimmed edge, put the blouse on the doll, then pull up the gathers to fit the neck and fasten off. Space out the gathers evenly all round. Now sew the tops of the arms to the doll's body at each side taking the stitches through the blouse fabric.

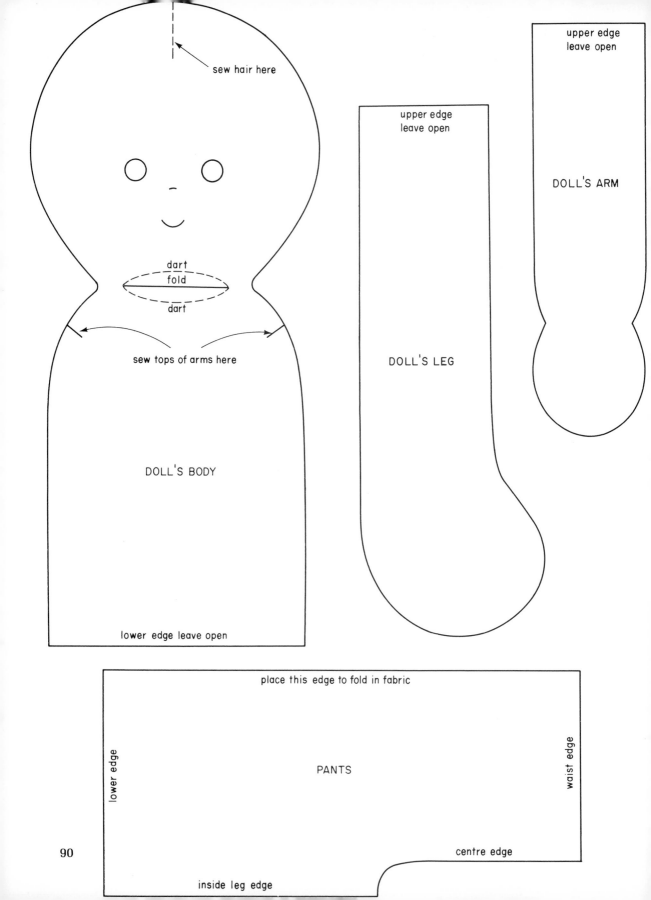

sew hair here

DOLL'S ARM

upper edge
leave open

upper edge
leave open

dart
fold
dart

DOLL'S LEG

sew tops of arms here

DOLL'S BODY

lower edge leave open

place this edge to fold in fabric

lower edge

PANTS

waist edge

90

centre edge

inside leg edge

Rag doll in pants and blouse

Rag doll in blouse and skirt

For each sleeve cut a 6 cm by 12 cm (2½ in. by 4¾ in.) strip of plain fabric. Join the short edges of each strip, then turn in the remaining raw edges and press. Sew lace edging to one of these edges. Run gathering threads round both edges and slip a sleeve over each arm. Pull up the gathers in the lace-trimmed edges to fit the arms then fasten off. Slip stitch these edges of the sleeves to the bodice all round the arm.

To make the pants

Cut two pants pieces from plain fabric, placing the edge indicated on the pattern to a fold in the fabric. Turn in the lower leg edges 5 mm (¼ in.) twice and stitch, forming a casing for the elastic. Sew lace edging to the edges of the casings. Thread elastic through each casing to fit round the doll's legs and secure the elastic at each side of the casing with a stitch or two.

Join the pants pieces to each other at the centre edges then clip the curves in the seams. Bring these seams together, then join the inside leg edges of each pants piece. Make a narrow casing for the

elastic at the waist edge in the same way as for the leg edges, then thread through elastic to fit the waist.

To make the skirt

Cut a 17 cm by 44 cm (6¾ in. by 17½ in.) strip of plain fabric. Join the short edges leaving 6 cm (2½ in.) of the seam open at one end for the back waist opening. Turn in the raw edges of the opening and stitch them down to neaten. Hem and trim the lower raw edge with lace edging. Gather the remaining raw edge to measure 17 cm (6¾ in.) and bind it with a 3 cm by 18 cm (1¼ in. by 7 in.) strip of fabric for the waistband. Sew a snap fastener to the ends of the waistband.

To make the apron

Cut an 11 cm by 44 cm (4¼ in. by 17½ in.) strip of patterned fabric. Make in the same way as given for the skirt, but use a 4 cm by 18 cm (1½ in. by 7 in.) strip of fabric for the waistband, and do not hem and trim the lower edge with lace. For the hem frill, cut a 5 cm (2 in.) wide strip of fabric about 66 cm (26 in.) in length. Hem one long edge of the frill, then gather the other edge to fit the lower edge of the apron and sew it in place.

For the shoulder straps cut two 4 cm by 9 cm (1½ in. by 3½ in.) strips of fabric. Join the long edges of each strip then turn them right side out. Sew the ends of the straps to the inside of the apron waistband to pass over the doll's shoulders as shown in the illustration.

To make the cap
Cut a 7 cm by 30 cm (2¾ in. by 12 in.) strip of plain fabric. Join the short edges of the strip. Turn in one long edge and sew on lace edging. Run a gathering thread round the remaining raw edge, pull up the gathers very tightly and finish off. Turn the cap right side out. Run a gathering thread round the edge of the cap where the lace is stitched on. Pull up the gathers to make the cap fit on the doll's head just behind the hair, then finish off the thread. Put a little stuffing inside the cap to shape it, then catch it to the head all round through the gathers. Make a small bow from patterned fabric and sew it to the front of the cap.

Teddy in a carry-cot

The teddy is about 16 cm (6¼ in.) in height and the carry-cot measures 20 cm by 10 cm by 5 cm (8 in. by 4 in. by 2 in.). The carry-cot or baby carrier, made of quilted fabric, is complete with mattress, padded quilt and a pillow. The teddy is made by the stitch-around method. Seam allowance and turnings are given in the instructions for each item.

Materials required for the teddy
Small pieces of fawn fleecy fabric, striped cotton fabric, stuffing, felt and ribbon
Adhesive

To make the teddy
Trace the body, head and ear patterns off the page

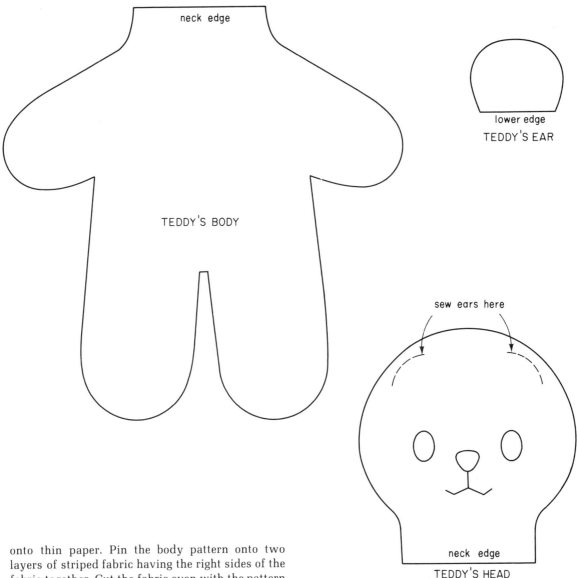

neck edge

lower edge

TEDDY'S EAR

TEDDY'S BODY

sew ears here

neck edge

TEDDY'S HEAD

onto thin paper. Pin the body pattern onto two layers of striped fabric having the right sides of the fabric together. Cut the fabric even with the pattern at the neck edge. Stitch all round close to the edge of the pattern leaving the neck edges open. Remove the paper pattern and cut out the body 3 mm (⅛ in.) away from the stitching line. Turn the body right side out and stuff. Run a gathering thread round the neck edge then pull up the gathers tightly and finish off.

Make the head in the same way as given for the body, using fleecy fabric. Place the head on top of the body, matching the seams at each side, then ladder stitch the head and body securely together where they touch.

Pin the ear pattern onto two layers of fleecy fabric having the right sides of the fleece together.

Trim the fleece even with the lower edge of the pattern then stitch and cut out the ear as for the body. Turn right side out and oversew the lower raw edges of each ear together. Sew the lower edges of the ears to the positions shown on the head pattern.

Cut the eyes and nose from black felt and glue them in place as shown. Work the mouth in straight stitches below the nose using black thread. Tie a ribbon bow round the neck. Finally sew three tiny circles of felt down the front of the body for buttons working a cross stitch in the centre of each one.

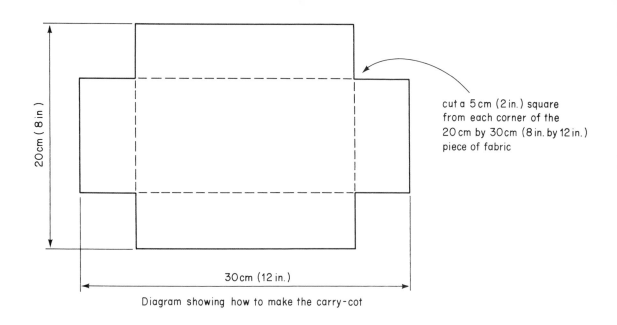

cut a 5 cm (2 in.) square
from each corner of the
20 cm by 30 cm (8 in. by 12 in.)
piece of fabric

20 cm (8 in.)

30 cm (12 in.)

Diagram showing how to make the carry-cot

Materials required for the carry-cot

A piece of quilted fabric measuring 20 cm by 30 cm (8 in. by 12 in.) for the carry-cot

A piece of cotton fabric for the lining and carrying straps measuring 24 cm by 40 cm (9½ in. by 16 in.)

Two 11 cm by 21 cm (4½ in. by 8½ in.) pieces of quilted fabric for the mattress

Small pieces of cotton fabric, lace edging and stuffing for the pillow and quilt

To make the carry-cot

Cut a 5 cm (2 in.) square from each corner of the carry-cot fabric as shown in the diagram. Fold over and press the fabric along the dotted lines shown on the diagram, having the right side of the fabric outside. Stitch through each of the folds close to the edge. Turn the carry-cot wrong side out and bring the 5 cm (2 in.) edges together at each corner. Stitch across the cut edges at each corner taking tiny seams, thus forming the box-shape. Turn the carry-cot right side out.

For the lining cut a 24 cm by 34 cm (9½ in. by 13½ in.) piece of fabric. Cut a 7 cm (2¾ in.) square from each corner of the fabric in the same way as for the carry-cot. Stitch the lining in the same way as for the carry-cot. Place the lining inside the carry-cot having the wrong sides of the fabrics together, then pin the lining to the quilted fabric at all the corners. Turn in the raw edges of the lining 5 mm (¼ in.) then turn these edges down over the quilted fabric and slip stitch in place all round. Pinch each corner of

the carry-cot at the upper edge to make a sharp right angle, then oversew the lining at each corner to hold it in this position.

For each carry strap cut a 3 cm by 18 cm (1¼ in. by 7 in.) strip of fabric. Fold in all the raw edges 5 mm (¼ in.) and press, then fold the strip in half along the length and press, having the right side of the fabric outside. Stitch through all the edges of the straps as folded. Sew a strap to each side of the carry-cot as illustrated.

Join the mattress pieces round the edges taking a 5 mm (¼ in.) seam, rounding off all the corners and leaving a gap for turning. Trim the corners, turn the mattress right side out and slip stitch the gap.

For the pillow cut two 9 cm by 11 cm (3½ in. by 4½ in.) pieces of fabric. Make as given for the mattress but push in a little stuffing before slip stitching the gap. Sew lace edging all round the edges.

For the quilt cut two 11 cm (4½ in.) squares of fabric and make as for the pillow.

Top **'Cries of London' peg dolls**

Bottom **Three bears cottage**

Santa and Mrs Claus at home

These fabric rosette dolls are each 30 cm (12 in.) in height and their squashy armchairs, made from fleecy fabric and wadding are 17 cm (6½ in.) high. The green fur fabric Christmas tree measures 30 cm (12 in.)

Pink cotton knit (stockinette) fabric is used for the dolls' heads and hands, and should this be difficult to obtain, cuttings off an old white T-shirt can be used instead. The T-shirt fabric can be tinted pink if desired with cold water dye or it can be left white. Seams and turnings of 5 mm (¼ in.) are allowed on all pieces unless otherwise stated. Make the fabric rosettes as explained at the beginning of the book.

Materials required for the dolls
For the heads and hands, small pieces of pink cotton knit (stockinette) fabric or cuttings off a T-shirt

Small amount of stuffing

Small pieces of black felt for the boots

Scraps of black and red felt, red thread and red pencil for the facial features

Thin round elastic, 90 cm (1 yd) in length, for each doll

Small ball of white knitting wool for the hair

For Santa Claus, remnants of plain red fabrics and white fur fabric

For Mrs Claus, remnants of red patterned fabrics, white fabric and 50 cm (20 in.) of white lace edging

Adhesive

To make Santa Claus

Cut out and gather plain red fabric circles of the following diameters. For the body: four 16 cm (6¼ in.), two 17 cm (6⅝ in.), two 18 cm (7 in.), two 19 cm (7½ in.) and two 20 cm (8 in.). For each leg: eight 12 cm (4¾ in.). For each arm: eight 10 cm (4 in.) and six 9 cm (3½ in.).

For the head cut a 12 cm by 18 cm (4¾ in. by 7 in.) strip of stockinette fabric, having the 'most stretch' in the fabric going across the 12 cm (4¾ in.) width. Join the 18 cm (7 in.) edges. Run a gathering thread round one remaining raw edge, pull up the gathers tightly and fasten off securely. Turn the head right side out and stuff to make a ball-shape measuring 26 cm (10¼ in.) around. Note that the seam will be at the back of the head.

Run a gathering thread round 1 cm (⅜ in.) from the remaining raw edge then pull up the gathers a little and turn in the raw edge. Cut a 60 cm (24 in.) length of elastic for the body, fold it in half, then tie a knot close to the folded end. Push this knot inside the head, pull up the gathers tightly and finish off, oversewing through the elastic to secure it.

Now thread three 16 cm (6¼ in.) circles onto the double elastic, then pass the remaining 30 cm (12 in.) length of elastic between the double elastic for the arms. Continue threading circles onto the double body elastic as follows: one 16 cm (6¼ in.), two 17 cm (6⅝ in.), two 18 cm (7 in.), two 19 cm (7½ in.) and two 20 cm (8 in.).

For the fur trimming at the lower end of the body, cut two 11 cm (4¼ in.) diameter circles of white fur fabric. Join them round the edges leaving a gap for turning. Turn right side out, then slip stitch the gap. Now use a darning needle to thread each of the body elastics through this circle, keeping the elastics about 3 cm (1¼ in.) apart on either side of the centre of the circle.

Thread eight 12 cm (4¾ in.) circles onto each elastic for the legs. For the fur trimming on each leg

cut two 7 cm (2¾ in.) diameter circles of white fur fabric. Make these in the same way as for the fur trimming on the body. Thread a leg elastic through the centre of each fur fabric circle, then knot the end of each elastic securely, trimming off any excess length.

For each boot cut two boot pieces from black felt. Join the pieces in pairs leaving the upper edges open. Trim the seams, turn the boots right side out and stuff. Gather round the upper edges enclosing the knots in the elastic at the ends of the legs, in the same way as given for the head.

Onto each end of the arm elastic, thread eight 10 cm (4 in.) circles then six 9 cm (3½ in.) circles. Make the white fur trimming on each arm as for the legs using 5 cm (2 in.) diameter circles. Cut four hand pieces from stockinette, having the 'most stretch' in the fabric in the direction indicated on the pattern. Join the hand pieces in pairs leaving the upper edges open. Turn and stuff the hands then knot the ends of the arm elastics and attach the hands in the same way as for the boots.

Cut the eyes from black felt and the nose from red felt. Glue the eyes in place 8 cm (3¼ in.) down from the gathered top of the head and 2.5 cm (1 in.) apart. Glue the nose between the eyes as illustrated. Colour the cheeks by rubbing with red pencil then

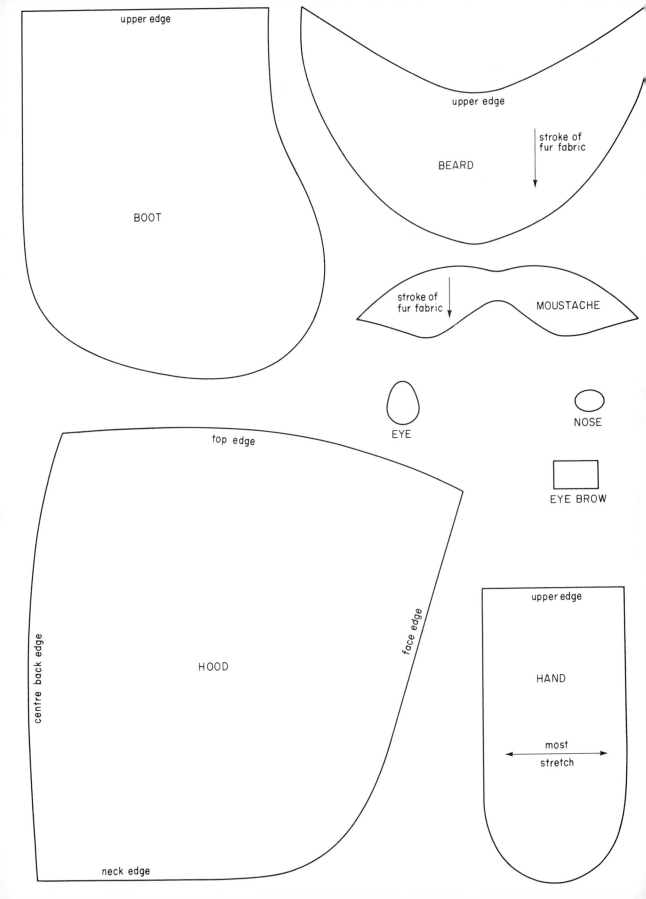

upper edge

upper edge

stroke of
fur fabric

BEARD

BOOT

stroke of
fur fabric

MOUSTACHE

EYE

NOSE

EYE BROW

top edge

centre back edge

face edge

HOOD

upper edge

HAND

most

stretch

neck edge

work a small U-shape for the mouth in red stitches 1.5 cm (½ in.) below the nose. Cut the eyebrows from white fur fabric and glue them above the eyes. Sew a few loops of white wool to the forehead. Cut the beard and moustache from white fur fabric, having the smooth stroke of the fur pile in the direction of the arrows shown on the patterns. Position the upper edge of the beard below the mouth, then sew this edge in place. Sew the moustache in position above the mouth.

Cut one pair of hood pieces from red fabric. Join them along the centre back and top edges. Turn the hood right side out and run a gathering thread round the neck and face edges. Put the hood on the doll, pull up the gathers to fit the head, lapping the hood over the beard slightly at each side. Fasten off the thread. Sew the raw edge of the hood to the head all round. For the fur trimming cut a 2 cm (¾ in.) wide strip of fur fabric long enough to go all round the edge of the hood. Sew one edge of this to the head, just covering the raw edge of the hood, then sew the other edge to the hood.

To make Mrs Claus
Cut out and gather fabric circles of the following diameters. For the body: two white 16 cm (6¼ in.), two red 16 cm (6¼ in.), two red 17 cm (6⅝ in.) and two red 18 cm (7 in.) For each arm: two white 9 cm (3½ in.), four red 9 cm (3½ in.), and eight red 10 cm (4 in.). For each leg: twelve white 11 cm (4¼ in.).

For the skirt cut a 16 cm by 50 cm (6¼ in. by 20 in.) strip of fabric. Join the short edges, hem one remaining raw edge and sew on lace trimming. Gather the remaining raw edge up tightly until the raw edges meet, then finish off.

Make the head as for Santa Claus, enclosing the knotted end of the double body elastic. Now thread two white 16 cm (6¼ in.) circles and one 16 cm (6¼ in.) red circle onto the double body elastic. Pass the arm elastic between the body elastics as for Santa Claus. Continue threading red circles onto the body elastic as follows: one 16 cm (6¼ in.), two 17 cm (6⅝ in.), and one 18 cm (7 in.). Pass the double elastic through the gathered edge of the skirt then thread on the remaining 18 cm (7 in.) red circle. Thread twelve 11 cm (4¼ in.) circles onto each elastic for the legs, then make and attach the boots as for Santa Claus.

Make the hands and thread on the arm circles as for Santa, placing the white circles next to the hands.

Make the eyes, nose and mouth as for Santa. For the hair, wind the wool into a small hank measuring about 30 cm (12 in.) from end to end. Tie the centre

of the hank with a bit of wool and sew the centre to the forehead 4 cm (1½ in.) above the nose. Take the strands down to the sides of the head and sew them there, then sew the looped ends to the back of the head.

Cut two 22 cm (9 in.) diameter circles of fabric for the mob cap. Join them round the edges leaving a gap for turning. Turn the cap right side out then slip stitch the gap. Run a gathering thread round the cap 2.5 cm (1 in.) from the edge. Pull up the gathers to make the cap fit just behind the hair then finish off the thread. Sew a small ribbon bow to the front of the cap.

Materials required for the Christmas tree
A piece of green fur fabric measuring 30 cm by 50
    cm (12 in. by 20 in.)
Small pieces of red felt, red fabrics, silver braid and
    card (thin cardboard)
One strand of Christmas tree tinsel
Small amount of stuffing

To make the Christmas tree
Make the pattern using diagram 1 as a guide. Draw out of a triangle to the size shown, then round off the lower edge. Cut out the tree placing the edge indicated on the pattern to a fold in the fur fabric. Join the straight edges of the tree then turn right side out

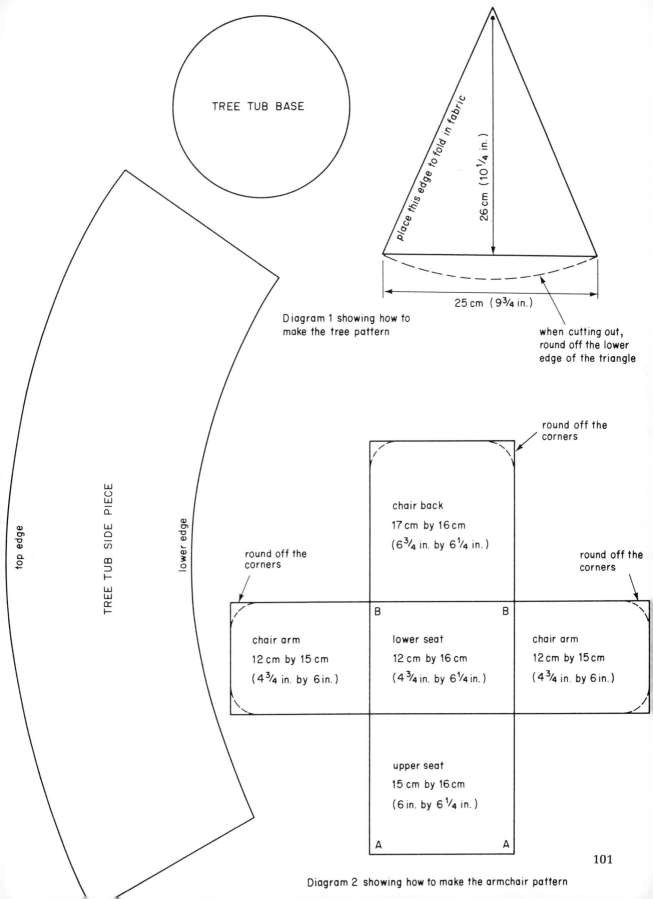

TREE TUB BASE

place this edge to fold in fabric

26 cm (10¼ in.)

25 cm (9¾ in.)

Diagram 1 showing how to
make the tree pattern

when cutting out,
round off the lower
edge of the triangle

top edge

TREE TUB SIDE PIECE

lower edge

round off the
corners

chair back
17 cm by 16 cm
(6¾ in. by 6¼ in.)

round off the
corners

round off the
corners

B   B

chair arm
12 cm by 15 cm
(4¾ in. by 6 in.)

lower seat
12 cm by 16 cm
(4¾ in. by 6¼ in.)

chair arm
12 cm by 15 cm
(4¾ in. by 6 in.)

upper seat
15 cm by 16 cm
(6 in. by 6¼ in.)

A   A

101

Diagram 2 showing how to make the armchair pattern

and stuff. Gather round the lower edge, pull up the gathers tightly and then fasten off the thread.

Cut the tub side piece and the base from red felt. Oversew the short edges of the side piece together, then place the base against the lower edge and oversew it in position. Turn the tub right side out. Put a circle of card inside the tub against the base then stuff the tub. Sew the top edge of the tub in place under the tree.

Trim the silver fringe on the tinsel a little shorter with scissors. Sew the tinsel to the tree as shown in the illustration. Make the balls from 4.5 cm (1¾ in.) diameter circles of fabric gathered round the edges and stuffed. Sew the balls to the tree and a rosette of silver braid to the top of the tree.

Materials required for one armchair

Two 50 cm (20 in.) squares of fleecy or other fabric
Two 50 cm (20 in.) squares of wadding
A little stuffing

To make the armchair

Draw out the pattern as shown in diagram 2. The easiest way of doing this is to draw out all the rectangular shapes individually then fix them together with clear (Scotch) tape to produce the required shape. Round off the corners at the dotted lines shown on the diagram.

Cut two chair pieces from fabric and two from wadding. Place the fabric pieces right sides together, with the two wadding pieces underneath. Join round all the edges through all thicknesses leaving the edge marked A-A open. Turn the chair right side out and push a little stuffing in the chair back and arms spreading it around evenly. Turn in the raw edges A-A and slip stitch, then fold up this flap and slip stitch edge A-A to line B-B.

Roll down the top edge of each arm to form the curved tops of the arms and slip stitch to hold in place. Bring the arms up and sew to the chair back where they touch. Catch the chair arms to the seat at the front where they touch.

For the chair legs cut out, gather and stuff four 7 cm (2¾ in.) diameter circles of felt. Sew one to each corner underneath the chair.

The man in the moon

The moon measures about 20 cm (8 in.) in length and it is designed to hang on the wall. The man in the moon is a finger puppet just 6 cm (2½ in.) high and he can be taken out of his window 'pocket'. Felt is used for making these toys and the finger puppet is made by the stitch-around method.

Materials required

For the moon, small pieces of felt in various colours, scraps of lace for the curtains, a short length of braid and a scrap of ribbon

For the man, scraps of pink felt for the body, red felt for the nightshirt and cap, a scrap of ribbon, a small bead, brown marker pen, stuffing, black and red thread, red pencil

Adhesive

To make the moon

Cut two moon shapes from felt then cut out the window from one of the pieces. For the window frame cut a piece of felt a little larger all round than the cut-out window, then cut the inner edge of the frame a little smaller than the window. Glue the window frame to the moon shape, then stitch it in place round the inner and outer edges. Cut a 6 cm by 8 cm (2¼ in. by 3¼ in.) piece of black felt and stick this to the other moon shape so that it is behind the window when both pieces are placed together. Stick bits of lace to this piece of black felt for lace curtains.

Cut the door from felt and work lines of stitching on it as shown on the pattern. Sew the door in place on the moon piece. Now join the moon pieces to each other all round, close to the edges, having the right sides outside. Cut the doorstep from felt and glue it in place, then glue braid round the outer edge of the door. Cut the letterbox and doorknob from felt and

glue them in place.

For the roof tiles cut 2 cm (¾ in.) wide strips of felt. Make 1 cm (⅜ in.) deep snips along one long edge spacing them at 1 cm (⅜ in.) intervals. Glue the first strip in place at the position shown on the pattern, turning and gluing the ends of the strip round the back of the moon. Glue the other tile strips in place, lapping them slightly over each other until the roof is covered. Sew a small loop of ribbon to the top point for hanging up.

To make the finger puppet

Trace the body pattern off the page onto thin paper then cut it out. Pin the pattern onto two layers of pink felt. Cut the felt even with the pattern at the lower edge. Stitch all round close to the edge of the pattern, leaving the lower edges open. Remove the pattern and cut out the body close to the stitching line. Stuff the head and arms, then sew through both layers of felt at the dotted lines shown on the pattern to hold the stuffing in place. Use brown marker pen to mark on the hair, then work the eyes in black stitches and the mouth and nose in red stitches. Colour the cheeks by rubbing with the moistened tip of a red pencil.

Cut two nightshirt pieces from red felt, then oversew the side edges together. Slip the nightshirt onto the puppet, then oversew or whip stitch the front and back shoulder edges together. Stick a tiny ribbon bow at the front neck edge.

Cut two nightcap pieces from felt and trim one along the dotted line shown on the pattern for the cap front. Oversew the side edges of the cap together then turn it right side out. Stick the nightcap to the head, and sew the bead to the top point. Bend over the point and catch it to the cap with a stitch or two.

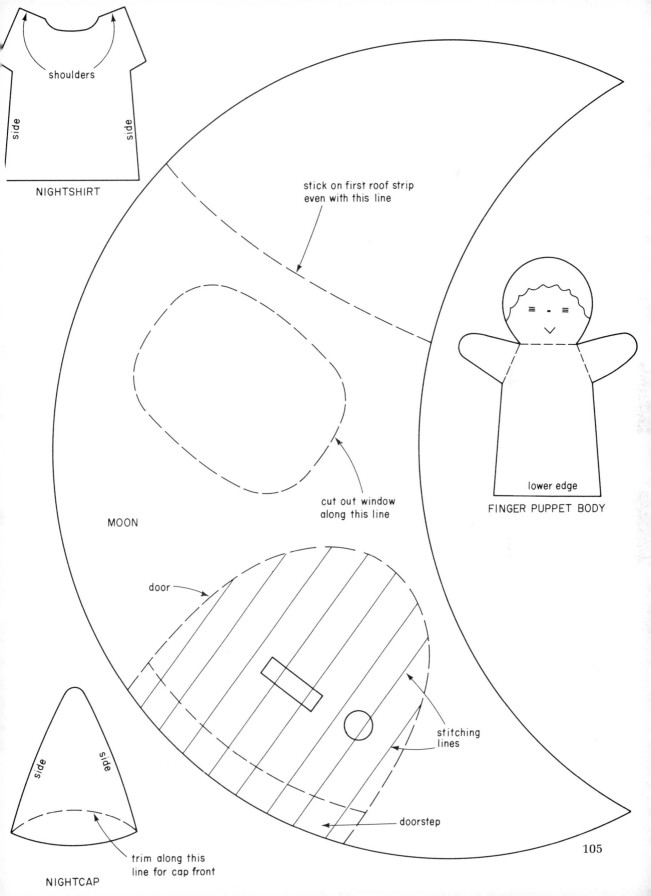

shoulders

side

side

NIGHTSHIRT

stick on first roof strip
even with this line

cut out window
along this line

MOON

door

stitching
lines

doorstep

FINGER PUPPET BODY

lower edge

side

side

trim along this
line for cap front

NIGHTCAP

105

Baby doll in a basket

Here is a toy guaranteed to delight any little girl. The baby doll, made from felt, has a complete layette of clothes for day and night wear. All the items fit neatly inside a bread basket lined with fabric, measuring 22 cm (8¾ in.) in diameter and 9 cm (3½ in.) deep. The lid is made from card (thin cardboard) to fit on top of the basket and it is covered with matching fabric.

The doll, made by the stitch-around method, measures 19 cm (7½ in.). The vest (or undershirt) and nappy (or diaper) are sewn in place on the doll, but all the other garments are removable.

Turnings of 5 mm (¼ in.) are allowed on all the garment pieces unless otherwise stated.

Materials required for the doll
Small pieces of flesh-coloured felt
For the facial features, black felt, red pencil and red thread
For the hair, small amount of 3 or 4 ply knitting wool
Small amount of stuffing
Adhesive

To make the doll
Trace the body, body base, arm and leg patterns off the page onto thin paper and cut them out. Pin the body pattern onto two layers of felt, then cut the felt even with the pattern at the lower edge. Stitch all round close to the edge of the pattern leaving the lower edges open. Remove the pattern and cut out the body close to the stitching line. Turn right side out and stuff very firmly, coaxing the head into a nice rounded shape. Cut the body base piece from felt and place it against the lower edges of the body, matching points A. Stretch one of the lower body edges to fit round the back edge of the body base piece. This edge will be at the back of the doll. Oversew (wnip stitch) the edges of the base to the lower edges of the body, adding more stuffing if necessary.

Tie a few strands of sewing thread very tightly around the doll's neck, then sew the thread ends into the neck. Use a pencil to lightly mark on the positions of the facial features as shown on the pattern. Cut the eyes from felt and glue them in place, then mark the eyelashes with pencil. Use the moistened tip of a red pencil to colour the mouth, nose and cheeks. Work three tiny red stitches across the centre of the mouth.

For the hair, take eight strands of wool about 1 m (1 yd) in length. Using matching sewing thread, sew the ends of the wool to the head at the position shown on the pattern. Take the strands down over the face and loop them round a pin pushed into the head at the position of the hair line as shown on the pattern. Take the strands over the top of the head towards the back of the neck and loop them around a pin pushed into the head about 1.5 cm (½ in.) above the neck. Take the strands back up over the head towards the front hair line and repeat the process described, a few more times. Now catch the wool loops to the head with matching sewing thread, removing the pins as they are sewn in place. Continue in this way until one side of the head is reached, then cover the other side of the head in the same way. To hold the wool strands in place on top of the head, back stitch them to the head in line with the doll's head seam. Make a tiny ribbon bow and sew it to the hair.

For the right leg, pin the pattern onto two layers of felt and cut the felt even with the pattern at the upper edge. Stitch the leg, cut out and turn in the same way as for the body. Stuff the leg firmly, but stuff a little more lightly at the top. Tie sewing thread round the ankle as for the neck. Now bring the top edges of the leg together, having the seams at the positions shown in diagram 1, then oversew the edges together. Oversew the top edges of the leg to the lower front edge of the body as shown on the body pattern. Make the left leg in the same way but

108

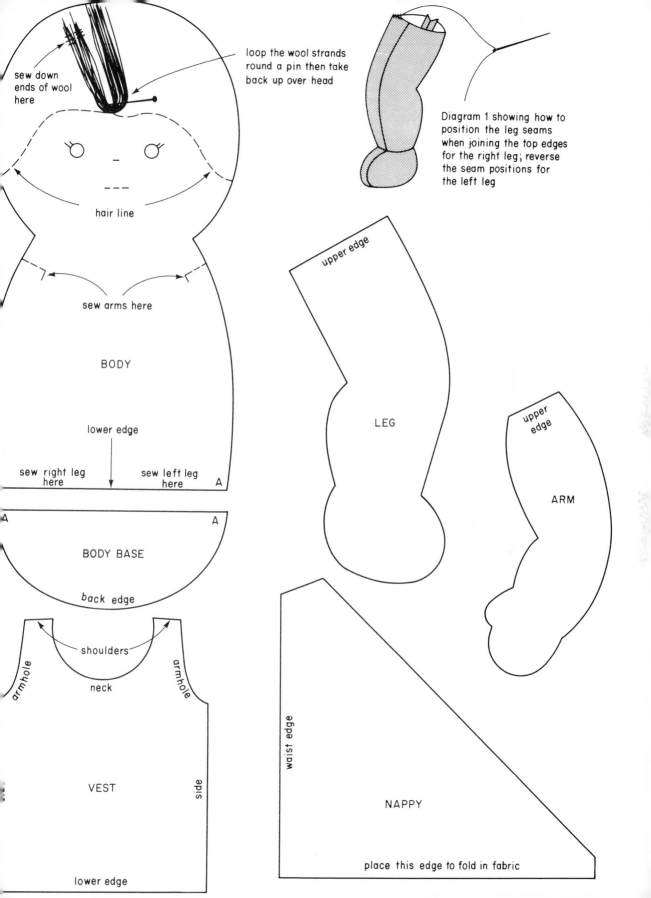

sew down
ends of wool
here

loop the wool strands
round a pin then take
back up over head

hair line

sew arms here

BODY

lower edge

sew right leg
here

sew left leg
here

A

A

A

BODY BASE

back edge

shoulders

armhole

armhole

neck

VEST

side

lower edge

Diagram 1 showing how to
position the leg seams
when joining the top edges
for the right leg; reverse
the seam positions for
the left leg

upper edge

LEG

upper
edge

ARM

waist edge

NAPPY

place this edge to fold in fabric

place the seams in the reverse position when sewing the top edges together.

For the arm, pin the pattern onto two layers of felt then cut the felt even with the pattern at the upper edge. Stitch the arm, cut it out, and turn it as for the leg. Stuff the hand and lower arm firmly then the upper portion more lightly. Tie thread round the wrists as for the ankles. Oversew the upper edges of the arm together, then sew it to the side of the body at the position shown on the pattern. Make the other arm in the same way.

Materials required for the clothes
Small pieces of thin soft fabrics, trimmings, lace edging, ribbons, stretchy fabrics such as cuttings off discarded socks, panties, vests, and T-shirts

Narrow elastic or shirring elastic

Two small hooks and eyes

To make the vest
Use stretchy fabric for the vest, trimming it with narrow lace edging. Cut out two vest pieces. Bind the armhole and neck edges of the vest pieces with the lace edging, folding the edging in half over the raw edges. Sew the lace in place with loose running stitches. Join the side edges of the vest, then place it right side out on the doll. Oversew the shoulder edges together neatly on the doll's shoulders.

To make the nappy
Cut the nappy from fabric, placing the edge indicated to a fold in the fabric. Turn in the raw edges and stitch all round. Fold the nappy around the doll and sew the corners in place at the centre front as illustrated.

To make the dress and panties
Cut one pair of panty pieces from fabric. Hem the lower edges, taking 5 mm (¼ in.) turnings twice to form casings for the elastic. Thread elastic through to fit the tops of the legs and secure at each side of the casings with a few stitches. Join the panty pieces to each other at the centre front edges. Hem the waist edge and thread through elastic in the same way as for the lower edges. Join the centre back edges. Bring the centre front and back seams together, then join the inside leg edges.

For the dress cut two 8 cm by 12 cm (3¼ in. by 4¾ in.) pieces of fabric. Sew trimming to each dress piece as illustrated. Join the 8 cm (3¼ in.) edges for 3 cm (1¼ in.) only, leaving the remainder open for the armholes of the dress. Turn in these armhole edges and stitch them down to neaten. Turn in the neck edges 1 cm (⅜ in.) and stitch 5 mm (¼ in.) from the

folds to form casings for the elastic. Thread elastic through the casings right round to fit the neck, then join the ends of the elastic. Make sure that the elastic will stretch sufficiently for the dress to be put on over the doll's head. Hem the lower edge of the dress and sew a ribbon bow to the front.

To make the bootees
Make these from the top portion of a sock. Trace the pattern off the page and cut it out. Pin the pattern to the sock, having the edge of the pattern indicated to a fold in the sock fabric, and the top edge of the pattern even with the top edge of the sock. Stitch the back seam close to the edge of the pattern. Remove the pattern and cut out the bootee close to the stitching line. Turn right side out and sew a small ribbon bow to the front.

To make the bib
Trace the bib pattern off the page and cut it out. Pin the pattern onto two layers of fabric. Stitch all round close to the edge of the pattern, leaving a gap in the stitching at the lower edge. Remove the pattern and cut out the bib close to the stitching line. Turn the bib right side out and press, then slip stitch the gap. Sew lace trimming round the outer edge and ribbon ties to the top edges. Stick a piece of trimming to the centre of the bib.

To make the tights
Make these from very thin stretchy fabric such as the type used for stretchy nylon panties. Cut out one pair of tights pieces. Join the pieces at the centre front and centre back edges, taking 3 mm (⅛ in.) seams. Bring these seams together, and join the inside leg edges and around each foot, taking 3 mm (⅛ in.) seams. Turn the tights right side out and hem the waist edges, taking 5 mm (¼ in.) turnings twice, and stretching the fabric as it is being stitched. Thread through elastic to fit the waist.

To make the shawl
For this, use a piece cut from a fancy knit or similar fabric. Cut a 25 cm (10 in.) square, hem the edges and sew on lace edging.

To make the bonnet
Use the top of an ankle sock for this. Cut 6 cm (2¼ in.) off the sock top and machine stitch all round 1 cm (⅜ in.) from the cut edges to stop the fabric laddering. Trim off the 1 cm (⅜ in.) close to the stitching. Run a gathering thread round the stitching line, pull up the gathers tightly and finish off, oversewing all the raw edges. Turn the bonnet right side

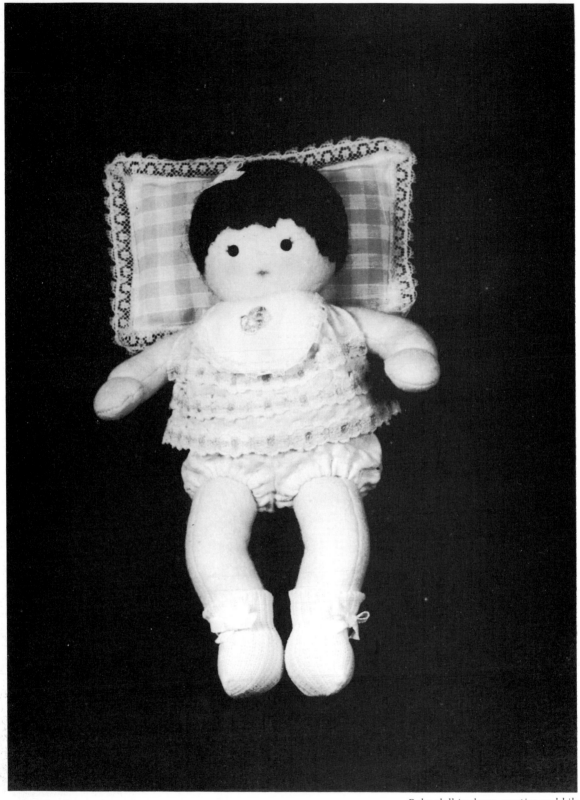

Baby doll in dress, panties and bib

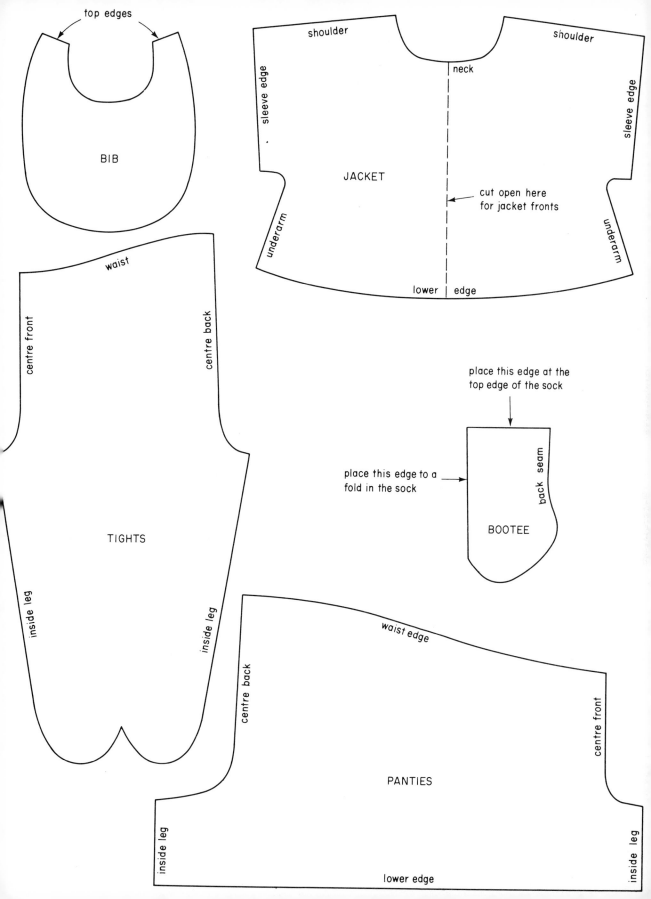

out and pull it onto the doll's head. Put a pin in each side of the bonnet close to the neck to mark the position of the ribbon ties. Remove the bonnet and sew on the ribbon ties and then rosettes made from ribbon. Sew lace edging to the face edge of the bonnet stretching the fabric slightly as it is being stitched in place.

To make the jacket
Use a non-fray fabric such as brushed nylon for the jacket. Cut two jacket pieces, then cut one of the pieces open at the dotted line indicated for the jacket fronts. Join the fronts to the back at the shoulders. Sew trimming to the sleeve edges then join the underarm seams. Turn the jacket right side out and sew trimming to the centre front and lower edges. Finally sew trimming round the neck edge and a ribbon tie to each neck edge at the centre front.

To make the nightdress
Trace the yoke pattern off the page onto thin paper then cut it out. Pin the pattern onto two layers of fabric then stitch all round close to the edge of the pattern, leaving a gap in the stitching at the front of the yoke as shown on the pattern. Remove the pattern and cut out the yoke close to the stitching line. Turn the yoke right side out and then slip stitch the opening. Press the yoke and sew lace edging round the outer edges.

For the nightdress skirt cut a 16 cm by 28 cm (6¼ in. by 11 in.) strip of fabric. Sew on trimming about 4 cm (1½ in.) away from one 28 cm (11 in.) edge. This is the hem edge of the skirt. Join the 16 cm (6¼ in.) edges for 9 cm (3½ in.) only, leaving 7 cm (2¾ in.) open at the top of the seam for the back opening. Turn in the raw edges of the back opening and stitch down to neaten. Turn up the hem edge 2 cm (¾ in.) and press, then turn in the raw hem edges and slip stitch in place.

Turn the skirt right side out. Turn in the remaining raw edge and run round a gathering thread. Pull up the gathers to fit round the doll's chest loosely, then fasten off. Space out the gathers evenly all round, then lap the front edge of the yoke a little over the gathers at the front of the skirt and slip stitch in place. Lap and stitch the back edges of the yoke over the skirt at the back in the same way. This should leave a gathered portion of the skirt at each side which will pass underneath the doll's arms.

Sew on a ribbon bow at the front, then glue on small guipure flowers or other trimming. Sew the hooks and eyes to the back edges of the yoke.

Materials required for the basket
An open basket of the type used for bread rolls, measuring about 22 cm (8¾ in.) in diameter and 9 cm (3½ in.) deep

Fabric, 60 cm (24 in.) in length and 91 cm (36 in.) wide, for lining the basket

Corrugated reinforced card cut from grocery boxes for making the lid

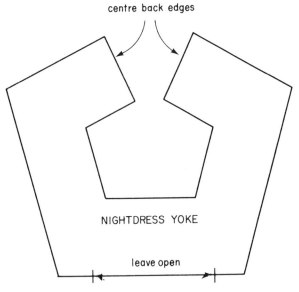

centre back edges

NIGHTDRESS YOKE

leave open

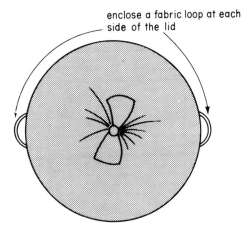

enclose a fabric loop at each side of the lid

Diagram 2 showing the loops for the ribbon ties

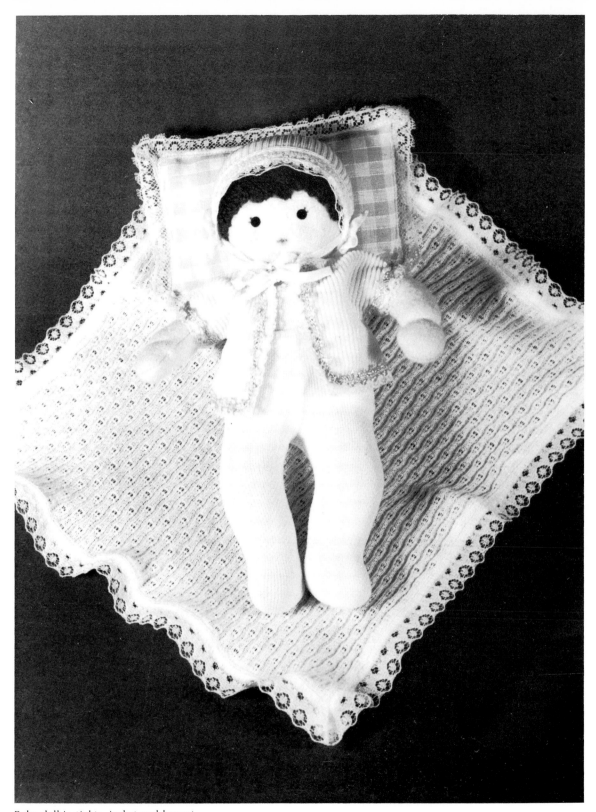

Baby doll in tights, jacket and bonnet

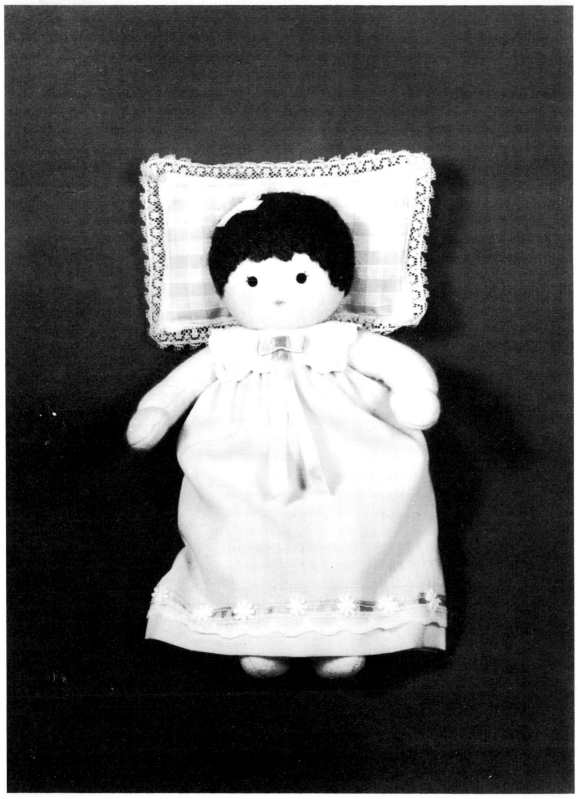

Baby doll in nightdress

A small piece of contrasting fabric for trimming the lid

Narrow elastic for the loops to hold the garments in place on the lid

Wadding or cotton wool, for padding the lid

Lace edging for the pillow

Adhesive

To make the lid

For the inner portion of the lid, cut a circle of card to fit the top of the basket. Place the card in the centre of a fabric circle cut 2 cm (¾ in.) larger all round than the card. Turn and glue the 2 cm (¾ in.) extra fabric onto the other side of the card all round. Now, on the fabric-covered side of the card, arrange a few items of the doll's clothing as shown in the illustration, and mark the positions for the elastic loops which will hold the garments in place. Using a darning needle, take lengths of elastic through the card at these positions and knot the ends together on the other side of the card.

For the outer portion of the lid, cut a circle of card and cover it with fabric as for the inner portion, but place a layer of wadding or cotton wool between the fabric and the card before gluing the edges of the fabric in place. For the lid handle, make a small bow from the contrasting fabric and sew it to the centre, taking the stitches through the card and pulling them tightly to depress the bow into the padded lid.

Now assemble both portions of the lid by sticking the wrong sides together, at the same time enclosing a loop made from ribbon or fabric at each side as shown in diagram 2. These loops are for the ribbon ties to pass through to hold the lid in position. Note that clothes pegs can be used to clip the lid pieces firmly together all round the edges until the adhesive is dry. Make gathered ruffles of fabric and sew these round the lid as illustrated.

To line the basket

First make the ribbon ties. For each one cut an 8 cm by 50 cm (3 in. by 20 in.) strip of fabric. Fold each strip along the length, and join the long edges and across one short end. Turn the strips right side out using a knitting needle, then press. Place a tie in the basket at each side to match the positions of the loops on the lid, having the short ends of the ties resting about 1 cm (⅜ in.) along the base of the basket. Catch these ends neatly in place, sewing through the base of the basket, then catch the ties to the basket again close to the top edge.

For the basket lining frill, cut strips of fabric the depth of the basket plus 4 cm (1½ in.), sewing them together to make a length of one and a half times the circumference of the basket. Turn in one long edge of the strip 2 cm (¾ in.) and press, then use a sewing machine to gather the strip 1 cm (⅜ in.) from the folded edge. Place the strip inside the basket around the side, having the gathered edge of the strip even with the top. If the strip is too long, trim the length, then join the ends of the strip. Gather the remaining raw edge to the same size as the other edge. Place the frill inside the basket, having the gathered raw edge on the base, then glue the top edge in place all round inside the top edge of the basket. Glue the remaining gathered edge of the frill to the base of the basket, smoothing down the fabric evenly all round.

To cover the inside of the basket base, cut a circle of card to fit, and pad and cover it with fabric as for the outer portion of the lid. Glue the base piece in place inside the basket to cover the raw edges of the lining frill.

To make the pillow, join two 8 cm by 13 cm (3¼ in. by 5 in.) pieces of fabric round the edges, leaving a gap for turning. Turn and stuff with wadding, then slip stitch the gap. Sew lace edging round the outer edges.

Furry families

These minature owls and rabbits are all easy to make from gathered circles of fur fabric filled with stuffing. The mothers and fathers stand 6 cm (2½ in.) high (excluding the height of the ears) and the babies measure 4.5 cm (1¾ in.).

If the fur fabric pile is too long it can be trimmed a little shorter by clipping all over with scissors. When gluing the felt pieces onto the toys, hold them in place with pins until the adhesive is dry.

The dotted lines on all the pattern pieces are the cutting lines for the babies.

Materials required for the toys
Scraps of fur fabric, ribbons, braids, felt trimmings and black thread
A little stuffing
Red pencil
Adhesive

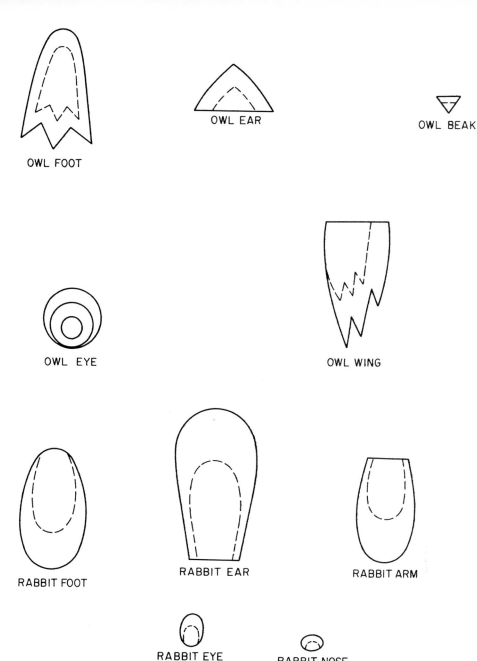

OWL FOOT

OWL EAR

OWL BEAK

OWL EYE

OWL WING

RABBIT FOOT

RABBIT EAR

RABBIT ARM

RABBIT EYE

RABBIT NOSE

To make the owls

For father owl's body cut a 10 cm (4 in.) diameter circle of fur fabric. Run a gathering thread all round the edge, then pull up the gathers, stuffing the circle at the same time. Finish off the thread.

For the head cut an 8 cm (3¼ in.) diameter circle and make as for the body. Place the head on top of the body with the gathered edges together, then ladder stitch them together all round where they touch.

For father's jacket cut a 15 cm (6 in.) length of 2.5 cm (1 in.) wide ribbon. Turn in the ends a little and glue them down to neaten. Gather one edge of the ribbon round the owl's neck so that the ends of the ribbon are 2 cm (¾ in.) apart at the front. Sew the gathered neck edge in place, then stick a ribbon bow to the front.

Trim the fur fabric a little shorter over the face area. Cut the feet from felt and position them under the body as illustrated. Glue the feet in place. Cut the ears from felt and glue them in place as illustrated. Cut three circles of felt for each eye, making each one a different colour. Glue them together, then glue the eyes in place. Stick two layers of felt together and cut out the beak, then glue it in place.

Cut one pair of wing pieces from felt. Stick narrow strips of ribbon round the top of each wing to match the ribbon used for the jacket. Glue the wings in place as illustrated.

For the monocle, make a circle of narrow gold gift wrapping braid a little larger than the eye pattern, glue the end in place, then leave an extra length at the other end for the chain. Glue the monocle between the owl's eyes only, then glue the end of the chain behind the neck bow.

Make mother owl in the same way as father, but gather an 18 cm (7 in.) length of 3.5 cm (1⅜ in.) wide ribbon right round the neck, lapping and gluing the short edges at the back.

Make the baby in the same way as for father using a 6 cm (2⅜ in.) diameter circle for the body and a 5 cm (2 in.) circle for the head. Cut all the felt pieces by the dotted lines shown on the patterns. Use the small and medium eye circles, then cut smaller circles for the pupils at the centre. Sew a ribbon bow to the top of the head.

To make the rabbits

Make the rabbit family in the same basic way as the owls, using the rabbit foot, ear, eye, nose and arm patterns. Work small black stitches on the faces for the mouths as illustrated before sticking on the noses. Colour the insides of the ears at the base with the moistened tip of a red pencil.

For father rabbit's whiskers, sew strands of white thread through the front of the face. Stiffen the whiskers by stroking them with a little adhesive.